GRIEG

EDVARD GRIEG

GRIEG

by JOHN HORTON

Great Lives

DUCKWORTH
3 HENRIETTA STREET
LONDON   W.C.2

First published in 1950

Printed by Jarrold & Sons Ltd., The Empire Press, Norwich

CONTENTS

CONTENTS

INTRODUCTION

MUCH of the biographical material in the following pages is based on David Monrad-Johansen's *Edvard Grieg*, published at Oslo in 1934 and translated into English—with slight condensation—by Madge Robertson in 1938. I am also indebted to Professor Gerald Abraham and my fellow-contributors to *Grieg: a Symposium* (Lindsay Drummond, London, 1948) and especially to Miss Astra Desmond and Mrs. Kathleen Dale for their lists of the songs and piano pieces respectively. This work should be consulted for a full bibliography and details of Grieg's works in every category. Other important sources, including the principal collections of Grieg's letters, are mentioned in the select bibliography on page 105. I have to thank Professor O. M. Sandvik, Mr. J. Philip Kruseman, Mr. Max Hinrichsen (Peters-Hinrichsen Edition Ltd., 25 Museum Street, W.C.1), and Mr. Walter Hinrichsen (C.F. Peters Corporation, 1209 Carnegie Hall, New York 19, N.Y.) for permission to quote from Grieg's correspondence and from other material.

J. H.

CHAPTER I

1843–1862

THE family tree of Edvard Grieg provides a kind of epitome of the range and activities of the mercantile, professional, and official classes during two centuries of Norwegian history. His mother, Gesine Judith Hagerup, came of a family whose ancestry has been traced back to one Kjeld Stub, a man of great versatility and strength of character, who was first an army engineer, then a pastor, and finally combined the militant aspects of both callings by leading a campaign against the Swedes in the war of 1643–1645. The surname Hagerup was derived from a Bishop of Trondhjem who had been first the guardian and later the patron of Gesine's great-grandfather. Gesine's father was a Stiftamtmann or provincial governor, and thus a member of the administrative caste that looked to Copenhagen for the sources and maintenance of its cultural life. On the other hand, he was closely associated with Norwegian parliamentary government from its birth, was twice a member of the Storthing, and might have risen, if he had wished, to still greater eminence in the political world. On the father's side Grieg claimed Scots connections. Alexander Greig—to give the family name its original spelling—was

9

born in Aberdeen in 1739. There had been
vigorous intertraffic between Scotland and Norway
since the early days of the seventeenth century; in
the 'thirties a Dundee merchant, Peter Dundas,
had come over and settled in Bergen, and his son,
under the name of Pastor Petter Dass, had become
one of the earliest writers to describe the everyday
life of the Westland peasantry. Alexander Greig,
a hundred years later, was likewise attracted by
the commercial lure of Bergen, the more so since
the 1745 Rebellion had brought upon his native
country not only bloodshed but also a burden of
economic depression. Alexander prospered in
his new home. His abilities as a merchant soon
showed themselves, he was able to acquire a
lobster-exporting fleet of vessels, and at the age of
forty he assumed Norwegian citizenship, though
it is said that he kept in touch with Scotland by
returning there annually to take part in the Com-
munion of the Reformed Kirk. In 1803 he was
appointed English consul in Bergen, an office in
which he was succeeded by his son John and his
grandson Alexander, the father of Edvard Grieg.

J. C. Dahl, in his charming little view of Bergen
painted about two years before the birth of
Edvard Grieg, recorded an impression of the busy
town as it appeared to one who lived in it and
loved it. Red-tiled roofs and leaded cupolas peer
between and above the crowded masts of the
fishing and trading fleets; the mountains, seeming
to gather up the colours of sea and streets, close
in the background possessively, but not for-
biddingly, as though insisting on their share in the
community created by the hazards of nature and

the business of man. It is a picture that has its
verbal counterpart in a description[1] written in
1737 by Ludvig Holberg, another of the illustrious
sons of Bergen, who was born there in 1684. He
tells of the town as he knew it in his boyhood.
There is the same perspective of harbour, town
and mountain-mass (Ulrikken), the same vapour-
drenched atmosphere making play with colours
and shadows. Holberg speaks with affection of the
Strandgate, the causeway running along the sea-
front that Bergen merchants and their customers
might walk dry-shod in the heavy rains Bergen
knew only too well. It was still called Strandgaten
when Edvard Grieg was born there, at No. 152, on
the 15th June 1843. He was the youngest but one
of the five children of Alexander and Gesine Grieg.
In later days the composer used proudly to display
on his watch-chain a seal, bearing the crest of
the Scottish Greigs and the Norwegian Griegs—a
ship in stormy waters and the motto *At spes infracta.*

Edvard came into the world at a time of swift
developments in Norwegian art and literature.
The first phase of Scandinavian romanticism
occurred in Denmark with the writings of Oehlen-
schläger and Andersen and the early compositions
of J. P. E. Hartmann. Somewhat later, about
1830, the Norwegians discovered among their
own peasantry a lively and varied culture founded
mainly on oral tradition. The folk-tales collected
in the dales by Asbjørnsen and Moe, who were
inspired to undertake this great task by the success
of the Brothers Grimm in Germany, were being
published about the time of Grieg's birth. Inci-
dentally, it was in that very year (1843) that the

[1] Grøndahl and Raknes: *Chapters in Norwegian Literature*, 1923, pp. 18 seq.

Rev. John Broadwood published the first collection of English folk-song melodies. Ten years later, in 1853, appeared Landstad's collection of Norwegian Folk Ballads. In 1848 Aasen produced his Grammar of the Norwegian Folk Language that laid the foundation of New Norse, or modern Norwegian. In 1849 Ole Bull made his attempt, to which we shall refer again, to found a Norwegian Theatre in Bergen. At the same period linguists and historians were delving into the records of mediaeval Norway and bringing to light a wealth of stirring material contained in the sagas of the old Norse kings and in the Eddas, the repositories of Northern folklore and religion of the pre-Christian era. Grieg, then, was born at the height of the romantic movement in Norway; the poets Wergeland and Welhaven were in full activity; and by the time he had reached early manhood Norwegian literature had asserted its independence and giants, Ibsen and Bjørnson, had begun their rise to world fame. Grieg's career was to touch theirs at several points.

As usual at such times, enthusiasm for nationalism in art and letters began with a small group and met with considerable opposition. Only gradually did it make its way into the comfortable, conservative homes of the official and professional classes in the larger towns. The environment in which Grieg spent his childhood was a cultured one, and included a great deal of musical activity. Alexander was a keen concert-goer, and liked to recall hearing Liszt give a recital in London. Gesine was a highly trained musician; she had studied with Albert Methfessel in Hamburg, had become an accomplished pianist, and regularly gathered friends about her to practise part-singing and chamber music. Bergen prided itself on its musical life, to which two or three generations of the Hagerup and Grieg families had contributed. Niels Haslund, father-in-law of John Grieg (the composer's grandfather) had helped to found the Bergen Harmonic Society in 1769 and in the following year had become its president. This John Grieg himself was a member of the orchestra. But to these worthy people Norwegian folk-music was almost if not quite unknown. It is doubtful if Edvard met with half a dozen genuine folk-tunes in their natural state during his boyhood, though the family can hardly have failed to hear some of Ole Bull's adaptations of popular song and dance melodies. Lindeman's collection of folk-music was appearing in print in the early 'forties, and Gesine may have dipped into a borrowed copy; it is improbable that she possessed one, or Edvard would have drawn upon the collection much earlier than he did. The music for which Gesine had the greatest affection, and which therefore was the first to fall upon the boy's sensitive ear, was by Mozart, Beethoven, Weber, and Chopin— the last regarded as a somewhat advanced taste for that place and time.

When Edvard was about ten years old, the family moved two kilometres outside Bergen to the estate of Landaas, which Gesine Grieg had inherited from her father. Edvard and his brother John had to walk daily into Bergen to attend school. Long afterwards, in some autobiographical notes written in 1903 and called *My First*

Success, Grieg recalled how an early attempt at composition—*Variations on a German Melody*—which he had proudly displayed to his schoolfellows, had been treated with sarcastic comments by masters at this school. His experiences of academic institutions seem invariably to have been unfortunate. He was a shy, diffident boy, easily discouraged and yet silently contemptuous of pedantry and stupidity. He did not excel in school subjects; but he managed to acquire a forceful and fluent style of composition in his own language and in German.

In 1858 came the first turning point in Grieg's life, for in this year the family at Landaas had a visit from the renowned violinist, Ole Bull. The reputation of Bull as a performer is fast fading; but something still remains of his personal glamour, to use deliberately a much-abused word. From boyhood he combined a robust and active physique with abundance of romantic imagination. By the age of nine he had made such progress on the violin that he was allowed to join the Bergen Harmonic Society's orchestra, a special clause being inserted into the regulations to admit one so young. By the time he entered Christiania University he was well known as a brilliant and unconventional player with a flair for experimenting in technical and musical effects. After a fruitless attempt to obtain lessons from Spohr, Ole Bull wandered about Europe, giving recitals that raised him to the first rank of violinists of the day and undergoing the most astonishing and picturesque adventures. In 1843 he toured in the United States, where his success was even more spectacular.

Five years later he returned to Norway to carry out his cherished plan of founding a Norwegian theatre and academy of music. The theatre was opened in Bergen in January 1850. One of the first productions was Wergeland's last play, *Fjeldstuen*, an attack on those who invited the impoverished Norwegian peasantry to emigrate to America. Ole Bull himself was soon to take part in this movement; for after sinking much of his fortune in the Bergen enterprise, and failing to obtain a Government subsidy for it, he left Norway again in 1852 and attempted to set up a Norwegian colony, called Oleana, in Pennsylvania. This venture Ibsen was afterwards to ridicule under the name of "Gyntiana". It failed, mainly through the roguery of one of Bull's business agents, and in the autumn of 1858 he was back in Norway, and established on the estate of his family at Valestrand, on Osterøy. He soon called on the Griegs, who were his neighbours, entertained them with stories of his amazing career, and insisted on hearing Edvard extemporise at the piano. He urged the Griegs to send their gifted son to Leipzig to study at the Conservatory.

The Leipzig Conservatory, founded by Mendelssohn in the year of Edvard Grieg's birth, had already attracted, and was to continue to attract for many years to come, some of the best student material of Europe and the United States. But from the first Grieg found its spirit uncongenial. He was only fifteen—and still wearing a blouse, the schoolboy dress of the period—small for his age, and delicate in physique; he was homesick, shy of his fellow-students, and bored by some of his instructors. He so much disliked the mechanical teaching of Louis Plaidy one of his first piano professors, that he asked to be transferred to another member of the staff. With E. F. Wenzel, the friend of Schumann, and with Moscheles, a fine exponent of Beethoven's works, he fared better. His greatest disappointment was in the composition lessons he received, and in later life he was wont to lay at the door of the Conservatory his lack of success in handling the larger forms of music, and in mastering the subtleties of orchestral technique. It would be a mistake, however, to take at its face value all that Grieg uttered against the Conservatory in moments of discouragement. Doubtless his strongest recollections were of the ineptitude of Carl Reinecke's tuition, in the course of which he was directed to write a string quartet and an overture without any preliminary instruction in instrumental technique and style. But in *My First Success* he paid grateful tribute to others among his teachers: notably Moritz Hauptmann, who trained him to listen to the effect of what he wrote rather than to follow blindly the injunctions and prohibitions of the text-book.

In other ways the time spent at Leipzig was not unprofitable. Grieg met some interesting fellow-students, among whom Arthur Sullivan was one—at a performance of *St. Paul* they once shared Mendelssohn's manuscript full score—and there were many opportunities for taking part in the rich musical life of the town. An environment that allowed a young man, as it allowed Grieg, to hear Clara Schumann play her husband's works, to hear Wilhelmine Schröder-Devrient—even at the age of fifty-five—sing Schumann's songs, and to attend fourteen successive performances of Wagner's *Tannhäuser* was worth the cost of a few dull lessons.

Grieg's emancipation from the Conservatory took place in the spring of 1862. Two years earlier he had spent a summer in Norway to recuperate from an attack of pleurisy that burdened him with chronic infirmity for the rest of his life. But he had insisted on returning to Leipzig and completing the course. At the students' Easter concert in 1862 he took leave of professors and fellow-students with some of the earliest of his published works: the *Four Piano Pieces* (op. 1), dedicated to Wenzel and showing strongly the influence of Schumann and (particularly in the Mazurka, no. 3) that of Chopin, and the *Four Songs for Alto Voice* (op. 2), set to German words by Heine and Chamisso. Whatever may have been his feelings towards the Conservatory, it gave him its institutional blessing. His certificate of proficiency in various branches of study has been preserved, and indicates that he went out of the doors of the Leipzig Conversatory a well-equipped musician. Dannreuther, who was a contemporary of his at the Conservatory, remembered him after nearly forty years as "a slightly-built retiring youth, of a typical Northern physiognomy, flaxen hair, and large dreamy blue eyes, very quiet, self-absorbed and industrious. As a pianist he never laid much stress on technique, but his playing was always delicate and intelligent."

CHAPTER II

1862–1866

THE prospects of a young Norwegian composer,
however talented, in his native country and in the
middle years of the nineteenth century, were nar-
rowly circumscribed. His lot might indeed be
compared to that of an English musician beginning
his career about the same period, except that
England could offer university posts and cathedral
and large parish church appointments that gave a
measure of security and some scope for creative
work. Norway, with its small population and
comparatively undeveloped cultural life, could
support very few professional musicians. Ole
Bull's dreams of a national opera and ballet were
as far as ever from realisation. There was no good
orchestra in the country and the level of amateur
choral singing was not high. Unlike Sweden and
Denmark, Norway did not possess musical institutions—such as a permanent opera—supported by
the State. Most serious of all was the absence of a
musical tradition, apart from orally transmitted
folk-music; and even this attracted less attention
in the strenuous, materialistic middle years of the
century that it had a decade or two earlier, in the
first enthusiasm of the romantic revival. It must
be admitted that the same lack of a tradition still

hampers the Norwegian composer; whereas the Dane or the Swede can launch out upon a symphony or an opera, a sonata or a ballet, with a certain confidence derived from the activities of his countrymen in those fields since the eighteenth century the Norwegian has little behind him except folk-music influences—including of course those inherited through Grieg himself—which are difficult to fuse into the larger traditional forms of art-music.

It was fortunate for Grieg that he scarcely realised the isolation to which the unique character of his talents was to condemn him. His first task was to bring himself to the notice of his friends and fellow-townsmen as a finished product of what was accepted as the best musical training to be had in Europe. He might thus hope to gain pupils, be invited to conduct choral concerts, perhaps secure a church appointment, and write an occasional piece of criticism in the newspapers that were playing so important a part in the intellectual life of the country. Once a reputation had been established at home he might look farther, to Copenhagen and Stockholm, and ultimately to the more important centres in Germany and other European countries.

By the early summer of 1863 Grieg had appeared at a number of concerts in Bergen, playing among other things his *Four Piano Pieces* and taking part in a performance of Schumann's Piano Quartet; he had written a short choral piece (*Rückblick*) for the Bergen Harmonic Society; and he had applied for a Government grant to pay the expenses of a few months in Copenhagen.

The grant was refused, but Grieg's father lent him the money. Copenhagen was an attractive place for a young artist. It had its Theatre Royal, its lighter entertainments in the pleasant Tivoli gardens, and its more serious orchestral concerts, and it had a constellation of musicians and men of letters. Of the musicians, Grieg sought out J. P. E. Hartmann and Niels Gade. J. P. E. Hartmann, the doyen of Danish composers, was renowned not only for his virile stage music, which not improbably influenced Grieg in the composition of *Peer Gynt* and *Olav Trygvason,* but also for having written the first Danish symphony of the romantic period. He was to live on, hale as ever, to the age of ninety-five, dying in 1900. Only a few weeks before his own death in 1907 Grieg played over Hartmann's *Vølvens Spaadom* ("The Seeress's Prophecy"). Younger, but still more widely famed, was Niels Gade, the trusted friend and colleague of Schumann and Mendelssohn. In the year of Grieg's birth Schumann had written: "Even in the North of Europe we have already seen national tendencies revealing themselves. Lindblad in Stockholm has translated for us his old folk-songs, while Ole Bull, though not a creative talent of the first order, tried to implant among us the sounds of his homeland. And the important Scandinavian poets have lately given a powerful impetus to their musical brethren, if indeed the latter have not learnt from their mountains and lakes, their runes and northern lights, that the North has a language of its own. . . . In (Gade's) music, and especially in the *Ossian* Overture, we may observe for the first time the imprint of a definite Northern character." It was this distinctive touch of national colour, faded though it may seem to us to-day, that caught the attention of Schumann, Mendelssohn, and other members of the Leipzig group of German composers, and won for Gade his early successes. He was a good executive musician too, and deputised for Mendelssohn as conductor of the Gewandhaus concerts. Even to-day some of Gade's stronger works, like the *Ossian* Overture, the First Symphony in D minor, the cantata *Comala* and the ballad *Elverskud* might well be heard occasionally outside Denmark. But under the influence of his German friends Gade's "Scandinavianism" became watered down, and his later works have few traces of spontaneity or originality.

Gade had always been a prolific composer and prided himself on a mastery of large-scale forms. The young Norwegian who appeared before him with a few piano pieces and songs must have seemed to him something of a trifler. Grieg's course was plain. He must tackle a symphony at once, if he wished to emulate the achievements of the masters: Schumann, Mendelssohn—and Gade himself. Grieg's attempt to follow Gade's advice took the form of a Symphony in four movements, the manuscript of which, dated the 2nd May 1864, was discovered among his posthumous papers. There is evidence that the whole work was performed on more than one occasion up to 1867, when the composer withdrew it, marking the score "Not to be performed". The two middle movements, however, were published as *Two Symphonic Pieces* for piano duet (op. 14). In later

years it amused Grieg to point out that in the
Andante he had anticipated by several years a
motive from Brahms's Requiem (at the words
"Ich will Euch wiedersehen").

More fruitful in artistic results was Grieg's
meeting with the poet and story-writer H. C.
Andersen. The four *Melodies of the Heart* (op. 5), a
set of songs to poems by Andersen, have always
been among the most popular of Grieg's works,
including as they do "I love thee" (so often and so
irrationally sung in German as "Ich liebe dich")
and "Two brown eyes". Nothing could be more
sensitive than Grieg's musical treatment of the
Danish words in this latter song: but the whole
charm is destroyed if German diphthongs are
substituted for the original pure vowels. Further
settings of words by Andersen appear in the
Romances (op. 18); here again we find some of the
most attractive, if not the most original, of Grieg's
songs—"Wandering in the Woods", "The Hut", and
"The Rosebud", together with the sombre "Young
Birch Tree" to words by the Norwegian poet
Jorgen Moe, and the dramatic "Autumn Storm"
to words by Christian Richardt. This song later
became the basis of the Overture *In Autumn*.
Another Danish poet, Christian Winther, was the
author of the texts of another set of *Romances* (op.
10), which appear to be the earliest of all Grieg's
published songs. The *Six Songs* (op. 4), composed
during this "Danish" period, are settings of German
words, but in the elegiac melancholy of "Die
Waise" by Chamisso (no. 1) and "Das alte Lied"
by Heine (no. 5) betray the composer's Scandinavian sympathies. In "Wo sind sie hin?" (no. 6)

Heine's words recall the old English poem of
The Wanderer:

Es ragt in's Meer der Runenstein, da sitze ich mit
    meinen Träumen.
Es pfeift der Wind, die Möwen schrei'n, die Wellen,
    sie wandern und schäumen;
Ich habe geliebt manch' schönes Kind und manche
    guten Gesellen.
Wo sind sie hin? Es pfeift der Wind, es schäumen
    und wandern die Wellen.

To this Grieg responds with a stormy setting with
an elaborate piano part, the whole foreshadowing
the opening of the C minor Violin Sonata and the
Prelude to Act V of *Peer Gynt*.

In Denmark Grieg found not only poets for his
songs, but also the ideal interpreter of them.
Nina Hagerup, the eighteen-year old daughter of
his mother's brother and of a celebrated Danish
actress, Madame Werligh, was two years younger
than Edvard. She too had been born in Bergen,
but in early childhood had come with her parents
to settle near Helsingør, in Denmark. As a young
girl she possessed a beautiful voice which was
almost destroyed by an attack of whooping cough
and never recovered its full power, though fortunately its quality was unimpaired. Her inter-
pretive gifts continued to develop, and were a
source of inspiration to Grieg as a song-writer.
Nina and Edvard were betrothed in July, 1864,
not without opposition from Nina's parents, for
Grieg was still almost unknown and had no regular
source of income.

In other ways the summer and autumn of this

year were to be momentous for him. He was
already on the road to becoming a musician with
leanings towards Scandinavian romanticism. He
was now to be directed into the narrower and
more difficult paths of Norwegian nationalism. A
stay with Ole Bull in his country seat at Osterøy
brought him nearer to the traditional lore of the
peasant fiddlers with whom Bull was on intimate
terms. And walking one day in the Tivoli pleasure
gardens in Copenhagen he was introduced by Fru
Magdalene Thoresen, the mother-in-law of Ibsen,
to a yet more fanatical lover of all things Norwegian. This was Rikard Nordraak, to give his
name in the Norwegian form he affected, and by
which he is now invariably known, although the
family name was originally spelt "Nordraach" and
he was christened "Richard". Like so many of his
countrymen, he was half Danish by birth. He
was a cousin of Bjørnson, had written incidental
music for some of Bjørnson's plays, and with his
setting of the same poet's lines, "Ja, vi elske dette
lande", had produced one of the most stirring of
all national hymns. He was now twenty-two, and
had little more than a year to live. It may be
difficult for those who are not countrymen of
Nordraak to discover in the scanty remnants of his
work the unique talent often claimed for him.
There is no doubt, however, that his songs and
piano pieces do show many of the national traits
afterwards exploited by Kjerulf, Svendsen, and
Grieg. But it was chiefly his dynamic personality,
with all its naive egotism and dauntless enthusiasm
that overwhelmed all who knew him. "It is not
easy", wrote Erika Lie Nissen, the pianist, "to say

how Nordraak affected those he came into contact with. Naturally some people thought him an oddity, a bit of a crank; that happens to all geniuses. But as a rule his superiority was recognised. He resembled Bjørnson in that he filled a room as soon as he entered it. His strong personality, his somewhat angular being, had an overmastering effect. . . . His conversation had a particular enchantment. It was not that he was specially witty or amusing. He was not one of those with whom one does nothing but laugh. But he was interesting; he himself was interested in everything, and he knew how to interest others." Grieg came at once under the spell. Nordraak, exclaiming "Now at last we two great men meet", dragged him round to his lodgings and played him selections from his own works, and doubtless talked much of Norway and Norwegian folk-music, which he, like Grieg himself, had approached through the transcriptions of Ole Bull. The most penetrating comment on this meeting was made by Halfdan Kjerulf: "Well, one really can say Les extrêmes se touchent." The impulsive, enthusiastic, amateurish Nordraak, and the diffident, self-effacing, academically nurtured Grieg: the contrast was remarkable enough to suggest that their friendship was like the affinity of two unlike chemical substances. Somehow Nordraak gave Grieg the self-confidence he needed; he turned him from a student into an artist with a mission; he set him free from the inhibitions of his German training.

Grieg paid tribute at once to Nordraak in the four *Humoresques* for piano (op. 6). These pieces

can scarcely be called whole-heartedly Norwegian, so near are they in style to Gade's *Scandinavian Dances*, but they represent the boldest
attempt at national colouring that Grieg had so
far ventured to make. Nordraak gave the second
of them his highest praise: "I might have written
it myself." It is interesting to notice that the
opening phrase bears a resemblance to a folk-
tune, *Alle mann hadde fota*; if this is more than
accidental it is the earliest example of Grieg's use
of folk-song material. To this transition period
also belongs the E minor Piano Sonata (op. 7),
dedicated to Gade and exhibiting some close
parallels with Gade's own Piano Sonata in the
same key, as well as with Schumann's G minor
Sonata; and the first Sonata for violin and piano
(Op. 8, in F), dedicated to Benjamin Feddersen,
a Danish literary friend who was Grieg's host at
the time of composition, and who had also received
the dedication of the *Poetic Tone Pictures* for piano
(op. 3). Both the Sonatas are "Scandinavian"
rather than Norwegian; that is to say, they observe
a compromise between the German romantic
attitude towards sonata form, and a certain
sombreness and ruggedness of utterance that
marks them as distinct in idiom from the lyrical
suavity of Schumann and Mendelssohn. Walter
Niemann says of the Violin Sonata: "Its background
is the Danish landscape . . . Denmark's beech-
woods, blue lakes, and gentle twilight are felt as an
undertone to the whole work." As compared with
Grieg's later experiments, there is little audacity
in the harmonic or contrapuntal treatment. One
feels that the composer is unhappy with the form

he has chosen to work in, and is constantly falling back on stock devices—sequences, canonic passages and so on—to keep himself afloat. The Danish affection for courtly dance-forms—an affection derived from Gallic rather than Teutonic sympathies—comes out in the Minuet and Trio of op. 7, which is the most distinguished part of the work, and in the Gavotte and Minuet of op. 8. Yet the Minuet-trio of the latter work instantly recalls the double-stopping effects of the Hardanger fiddle, already exploited in the *Humoresques* and perhaps borrowed from the piano pieces of Kjerulf.

The early Sonatas are symbolic of the fact that Grieg still regarded himself as a member of the younger "Scandinavian" school. Even the fanatical Nordraak was prepared to make common cause with his Danish contemporaries, and before long Grieg, Nordraak, and the two Danes, Hornemann and Matthison-Hansen, had formed a society styled *Euterpe*, with the object of giving concerts made up entirely of the works of Danish and Norwegian composers. The songs to verses by the Norwegian poet Andreas Munch (op. 9) belong for the most part to this period. "The Departure" is notable for its dramatic organisation, and for the modal colouring that was to become so important a feature of the composer's later style.

But Nordraak's brief life was almost at its end, and Grieg was to see little more of him. The two friends had planned to spend a holiday together in Italy, and in May 1865 Nordraak went on ahead to Berlin, where he had found a congenial master

for composition in Friedrich Kiel. The following
October he was struck down by rapid consump-
tion. He battled against the disease for nearly
half a year, and died on the 20th March 1866.
Grieg, having followed Nordraak to Berlin, was
able to visit him frequently during the earlier stages
of his illness, but at the beginning of November
had to hasten on to Leipzig, where his two
Sonatas were to be performed at a Gewandhaus
concert. Letters passed regularly between the
friends, those written by Nordraak becoming
increasingly febrile and urging Grieg to return to
his bedside; but Grieg continued his travels and
spent the winter in Rome. There, in the Scandinavian Club, he met for the first time a famous
countryman who was to play no small part in his
career: Henrik Ibsen. There, too, he wrote the
Overture *In Autumn* (op. 11), based, as we have
already noted, on the song "Autumn Storm". The
opening bare fifths suggest some influence from
The Flying Dutchman; perhaps, also, from Gade's
Ossian Overture. The subsequent history of this
work may be summarised here. After Gade had
pointed out a number of weaknesses in the scoring
Grieg transcribed it as a piano duet to play with
Nina. In this form he entered it for a competition
arranged by the Swedish Academy of Music. To
his amusement, for Gade was one of the judges, it
was awarded a prize and included in the publica-
tions of *Musikaliska Konstforeningen*. In 1887 the
composer completely revised and reorchestrated
it for the Birmingham Festival. In its final form it
consists of an andante Introduction, a main
section based on the song, and a conclusion

making use of fresh material—described as a Norwegian Harvesters' Song—in the rhythm of a *springdans*.

A smaller, but far more characteristic work, was the *Funeral March in Memory of Rikard Nordraak*, written a few days after Grieg received the news of Nordraak's death. It contains passages of a harmonic boldness that foreshadows Ravel's *Pavane pour une Infante défunte*, and is undoubtedly the most original composition Grieg had so far produced. He himself cherished it, and gave instructions that it should be played at his own funeral. Some may find it hard to reconcile the poignancy of the Nordraak March, and the touching letter he wrote to the dead man's father after visiting Rikard's grave in Berlin, with his apparent callousness in leaving Nordraak alone at the end. But Grieg's conduct was surely understandable, if not excusable; he could not altogether neglect the claims of his professional work and the opportunities of making new friends in Germany and Italy, and there is the possibility that he did not fully realise how serious was Nordraak's condition. Nordraak was given to describing everything pertaining to himself, and in particular the symptoms of his illness, in the most remorseless detail,[1] and his friends may well have formed subconsciously the habit of discounting much of what he said and wrote. But all this was forgotten in the memory of his youthful sincerity and enthusiasm. "Here," wrote Bjørnstjerne Bjørnson in 1869, "Here was true clarity and force, a full,

[1] These passages are among the omissions in the English translation of Johansen's biography.

round sum of Norse melodies and Norse patriotism, Norse portraiture and anecdotage, Norse dreams and fairy-tales, and a swarm of plans for Norse operas and symphonies—here Grieg listened and learnt, here was he born anew."

CHAPTER III

1866–1871

GRIEG had still to solve the problem of earning a living in Christiania or Bergen. On his return from Italy he took lessons in organ-playing with his Danish friend Matthison-Hansen, and made enquiries about church appointments in Norway. He also applied to Bjørnson, who had been made director of the Christiania theatre, in the hope of obtaining the post of musical conductor there. He got Ibsen to support his application, and when it failed to bring a response he received a consoling letter from Ibsen, who prophesied that he was reserved for something better. For the present, however, there was nothing to be done but to tread the hard path of teaching and concert promotion. He began with a concert in Christiania, on the 15th October 1866, at which he played his *Humoresques*, his Piano Sonata, and with Wilhelmina Norman Neruda (afterwards Lady Hallé), his first Violin Sonata. In the same programme Nina Hagerup sang songs by Grieg, Nordraak, and Kjerulf.

Halfdan Kjerulf was the most distinguished of the older musicians practising in Christiania. He was born in 1815, a member of a brilliant family overshadowed by the menace of tuberculosis.

Ida, his sister, who died in early womanhood, had been betrothed to the poet Welhaven, and Halfdan had set a number of Welhaven's poems in a sensitive but rather colourless style that recalls the weaker songs of Mendelssohn. More original are his settings of verse from the peasant stories of Bjørnson, dating from about 1860: "Young Venevil", with its fascinating bird-calls, "Ingrid's Song", with its folk-atmosphere and waltz-lilt, and "Synnøve's Song", which deserves to be at least as well known as Grieg's "Solveig's Song" in *Peer Gynt*. "The Princess", too, is a powerfully simple treatment of the lyric familiar to us through the settings of Grieg and Delius. Of the rest of Kjerulf's music only a few slight but not uninteresting piano pieces are remembered; they almost certainly influenced Grieg in the composition of his *Lyric Pieces*. Ill health and frustration had soured Kjerulf's disposition, and his relations with Grieg do not seem to have been cordial; but Grieg always respected his talents, and on his death in 1868 exerted himself to start a fund to provide a memorial to Kjerulf and did much to make his songs more widely known.

Grieg's first enterprise as a concert-giver in the capital brought him favourable notices in the press, and led directly to his appointment as conductor of the Christiania Harmonic Society. By the spring of 1867 he had helped the critic Otto Winter-Hjelm to launch a Norwegian Academy of Music, had given further concerts, mainly of works by Scandinavian composers, and had gained a footing in his own country that seemed to justify his severing some of his ties with Copenhagen,

including the directorship of *Euterpe*, which he now
resigned. On the 11th June Edvard Grieg and
Nina Hagerup were married in Copenhagen, and
soon afterwards took up their abode in a flat in the
Øvre Voldgate, in Christiania.

Here, by the end of July, Grieg's second Sonata
for violin and piano (op. 13) was finished. Niemann
calls this the "Norwegian" Sonata; certainly its
fervent, eloquent opening seems to come directly
and passionately from the composer's heart. He
dedicated it to the violinist Johan Svendsen, one of
the most outstanding, and at the same time one of
the most disappointing figures in the history of
Norwegian music. He was about three years older
than Grieg, and like him had studied at the
Leipzig Conservatory. In October, 1867, he
revisited his native Christiania, conducted his
Symphony in D to a half-empty hall, and left again
for the warmer artistic climates of Paris and
Copenhagen. In 1872 he returned for a while to
Christiania, to share with Grieg the conducting of
the Musical Society. He finally migrated to
Copenhagen in 1883, as conductor of opera and
ballet at the Theatre Royal, and most of his later
compositions were of a light or occasional character. He lives in the modern concert repertory
mainly by his *Norwegian Rhapsodies*, his *Norwegian
Artists' Carnival*, and his two early Symphonies, all
of which show that he possessed at least one gift
that Grieg lacked: a sure and practical knowledge
of orchestral effect. Gerhard Schjelderup has
pointed out the temperamental distinction between the two men: "While Grieg liked the loneli-
ness of the Sørfjord and the Folgefond which

mirrors itself in the deep water, Svendsen loved
the life of the town. Paris especially stood for
him in a glory of youthful memories." Opposite
natures, however, proverbially attract each other,
and Grieg was always grateful for the moral support he gained from Svendsen's competence and
self-assurance: "He taught me to believe in myself
and in the power and privilege of individuality.
There was a period when, in Christiania, it was
regarded as a crime to be individual. But along
came Svendsen, and he was individual too; and so
the miracle occurred—from then onwards I also
was tolerated."

Unlike Svendsen, Grieg had small ability as a
conductor, but he had enough Norse—or possibly
Scots—doggedness to pursue his aim of making the
Norwegian capital more musical. When the
Philharmonic concerts had to be dropped for lack
of support, he took the risk of replacing them with
subscription concerts. When the orchestral players
raised their price, he arranged chamber recitals
instead. Besides his own works, and those of other
Norwegian and Danish composers, he introduced
important standard works—Mozart's *Requiem*,
Mendelssohn's *Elijah*, Schumann's *Paradise and the
Peri*, Wagner's *Lohengrin* (concert selections), and
Liszt's *Tasso*.

All this executive work left him no time for
composition. That had to wait until the holidays,
which the Griegs generally spent in Denmark.
It is clear that even yet Grieg had not identified
himself entirely with Norway. He still spoke of
settling in Denmark, or even in Germany, if a
suitable post came along, rather than remain to be

stifled by the Philistine atmosphere that prevailed
in his own country.

In June, 1868, the Griegs crossed to Denmark
with their baby daughter, Alexandra, and rented
a cottage in Søllerød, not far from Copenhagen.
In the mild and undisturbed surroundings of this
pleasant place Grieg produced the most successful
of all his larger-scale works: the Concerto for
piano and orchestra (op. 16). In style it looks
backward to the Leipzig tradition, and particularly
to Schumann, whose Piano Concerto—also in A
minor—clearly served Grieg as a model; but it also
gives a foretaste of Grieg's whole-hearted adoption
of a national idiom. The orchestration of the
Concerto was revised more than once, and in its
present form dates from the last years of Grieg's
life. Although there is no actual quotation of
folk-song or dance tune the whole work is im-
pregnated with the spirit of Norwegian popular
music. The rhythms of *halling* and *springar* which
play an important part in the second Violin
Sonata are again much in evidence. What is
more important, the folk idiom begins now to be
absorbed into the musical personality of the
composer. For example, the principal theme of the
first movement, divided between woodwind and
strings, that follows the opening flourish, is charac-
terised by short repeated or sequential phrases of a
type that becomes increasingly common in Grieg's
writing, and is at the same time a distinguishing
mark of Norwegian folk-tune.

A smaller, but in its way not less important
landmark in the course of Grieg's development
was the book of *Lyric Pieces* for piano (op. 12), the

first of ten sets published between 1868 and 1901, the whole collection forming, despite its unevenness, one of the most interesting contributions to pianoforte literature. The *Lyric Pieces* again owe something to Schumann, especially his *Papillons*, *Kinderscenen* and other pieces with imaginative titles, something also to Mendelssohn's *Lieder ohne Worte*, and not a little to Gade and Kjerulf. This first set bears evidence of the composer's increasing nationalist tendencies; thus no. 5 is called "Folktune", no. 6 "Norwegian", and no. 8 "National Song". This last cries out for words, which Bjørnson was soon to supply.

The autumn of 1868 brought with it a renewal of the struggle against indifference and parochialism in Christiania's musical life. Concerts were kept going with difficulty, and the Academy of Music showed symptoms of a rapid decline. The gloom was relieved, however, by a kindly letter from Franz Liszt, who, at the summit of his fame, never failed to keep in touch with any promising or original artist, no matter how young or how obscure he might be. The letter, like most of Liszt's international correspondence, was written in French:

Monsieur! Il m'est fort agréable de vous dire le sincère plaisir que m'a causé la lecture de votre sonata (oeuvre 8). Elle témoigne d'un talent de composition vigoureux, refléchi, inventif, d'excellente étoffe—lequel n'a qu'à suivre sa voie naturelle pour monter à un haut rang. Je me plais à croire, que vous trouvez dans votre pays les succès et encouragements que vous méritez; il ne vous manqueront pas ailleurs non plus: et si vous venez en

Allemagne cet hiver, je vous invite cordialement à vous arrêter un peu à Weimar, pour que nous fassions tout à fait bonne connaissance. Veuillez bien recevoir, Monsieur, l'assurance de mes sentiments d'estime et de considération très distingués.

29 Decbr. 68. Rome.   F. Liszt.

Unsolicited praise from Liszt meant to Grieg more than encouragement; a sight of the letter was enough to satisfy the Norwegian Government that a State bursary, enabling the young composer to travel abroad, would be justifiable. Even so, another year passed before Grieg could afford to leave his work in Christiania, a year full of sorrow, for Alexandra, the first and only child of his marriage, died soon after her first birthday. At length, in February 1870, the Griegs made their way for the second time to Rome; for Liszt was at this period of his life living in turn at Weimar, Budapest, and Rome, and at the moment was to be found in a monastery near the Forum. He received Grieg with even more than his usual urbanity, listened to the second Violin Sonata, the *Humoresques*, and the Nordraak March, all played on the piano by the composer, and a few days later, when Grieg visited him again, played through at sight the whole of the Piano Concerto. In a vivid letter to his parents Grieg described how Liszt rose to his feet and strode about the hall of the monastery in his excitement at the climax of the Finale, where for the normal G sharp in the melody of the second theme Grieg substitutes a G natural, thereby producing a modal effect. It reminded him, Liszt said, of something similar in the works of Smetana, the founder of Czech

national music and another composer who had
profited by Liszt's encouragement. His parting
words to Grieg were: "Go your own way, I tell
you; you have the ability. And—don't let anyone
frighten you." Thus Liszt, the greatest living
executant musician, strengthened the sense of
mission that Nordraak, the inspired amateur, had
implanted in Grieg's heart. And still further confidence was now to be given him from another
source; this time it was a man of letters who
recognised and called forth Grieg's individuality.

CHAPTER IV

1871–1875

ON his return to Norway, Grieg dedicated to Liszt a cantata for female voices, *Foran Sydens Kloster* (At a Southern Convent's Gate). The music was in a sentimental religious style now no longer tolerated, though Liszt would not have objected to it. The text was taken from *Arnljot Gelline*, a poem by Bjørnstjerne Bjørnson, with whom Grieg was to have much to do during the next twenty years. Bjørnson was at this time in the prime of his creative life. He was esteemed not only as poet and dramatist, but also as novelist, journalist, and orator. Like Ibsen, he was on the point of turning for his dramatic material towards problems of contemporary life, but as yet he had not exhausted the vein of saga-history and folk-lore that had yielded him so much treasure. His interest in traditional music was strong; in his folk-novels, *Arne* and *The Bridal March*, he gives spirited descriptions of dance and song among the peasant communities, and the charming lyric poems scattered through these and other stories have been to Norwegian song-writers what the verses of Tennyson and Housman have been to early twentieth-century English composers. Among the first of Bjørnson's musical partners were, as we

39

have already noticed, Rikard Nordraak and Halfdan Kjerulf. But now both these composers were dead, and Bjørnson looked hopefully to Grieg to take their place. The contrast between Grieg's shy, introspective personality and Bjørnson's self-confidence and impetuous energy was reflected in the absurd incongruity of their appearance: Bjørnson immense, hirsute, and eupeptic, Grieg small and frail. But the friendship that grew up between them was real and, in spite of a temporary estrangement, enduring. Some of Grieg's best songs, among them "The Princess", "From Monte Pincio", and the "Four Songs from *The Fishermaiden*" (op. 21)—a set that contains that magnificent example of music matched to words, "The First Meeting" (no. 1) and the impetuous "Thanks for thy rede" (no. 4)—are settings of lyrics by Bjørnson. *Bergliot*, a longer poem describing a tragic episode from the Saga of Harald Haardraada, was treated differently; in 1871 Grieg set it as a melodrama, for declamation (preferably by a woman's voice) with an effective and well-organised accompaniment for piano that he later scored for orchestra in 1885, when it was first performed in public with the actress Laura Gundersen as speaker. For the drama *Sigurd Jorsalfar* ("The Crusader") Grieg supplied incidental music. Author and composer were present at the stage production in Christiania on Independence Day, 17th May 1872. Grieg was reduced almost to despair by the efforts of a distinguished actor to sing the straightforward song allotted to him in the last act, and cowered miserably in his chair until Bjørnson revived him with a hearty thump on the back. Of the instrumental pieces written for this play the best known is the "Homage March", forming a prelude to the scene in which the brother-kings, Eystejn and Sigurd, are escorted to their thrones. Another March, used as introduction to the second act, was adapted from a piece for violin and piano composed two years earlier. An intermezzo, "Borghild's Dream", forms with the two Marches a suite of pieces revised and rescored from the stage version in 1892. Another joint work of Bjørnson and Grieg, the male-voice cantata *Landkjaending* ("Recognition of Land") was also performed for the first time on the 17th May 1872, in aid of a fund for the restoration of Trondhjem Cathedral. It is a virile, square-cut setting for baritone solo and male chorus of a poem describing the return of the Christian king Olav Trygvason to claim his rights in his native country.

By this time Grieg was an important figure in public life, and his stirring and sincere contributions to music that could be performed on national occasions were suitably recognised by authority. In 1873 he was created a Knight of St. Olav, and in the following year he and Svendsen each received a grant of 1,000 Kroner from the Storting. From this time onwards Grieg was to accumulate distinctions and decorations from universities, learned and artistic societies, and governments all over Europe. He accepted them all with a whimsical nonchalance; it amused his sturdy Scandinavian temperament to be addressed as "Doctor" and to have a layer of medals at the top of his travelling trunk with which to impress the customs officers.

About 1872 Bjørnson and Grieg began to plan
an opera. They tried first as a subject Bjørnson's
Arnljot Gelline, and a few sketches of Grieg's music
have survived. Then it was decided that a work
should be built, like the cantata *Recognition of
Land*, round the figure of Olav Trygvason and
designed so as to give scope for national colouring
in words, music, and scenic effect. The theme of
the story was to be the clash between the old Norse
paganism and the new Christian faith. The opening scenes were to be enacted in a temple of Odin,
where ritual chants and dances, led by a High
Priest and a Vølva or prophetess, would provide
the composer with opportunities for lavish use of
soloists, chorus, and orchestra. In July 1873
Bjørnson sent Grieg the first three scenes of the
text, and within a few weeks Grieg had set these
in piano score, and was petitioning the author for
the rest of the opera. At this point, however, there
occurred a series of delays and distractions, leading
to the breakdown of the project and, for a time,
the estrangement of composer and author. The
most probable explanation of the affair is that
Bjørnson, in turning towards realistic themes
from contemporary life (such as *The Editor* and
A Bankrupt) lost his interest in romanticised history,
whereas Grieg remained a romantic to the end.
However this may have been, Bjørnson was
indignant when he heard that Grieg had failed to
consult him before undertaking what he hastily
assumed to be another opera.

On the 23rd January 1874 Grieg had received
a letter from Henrik Ibsen, inviting him to supply
incidental music for the first stage performance of

his verse-drama, *Peer Gynt*. Grieg undertook the commission with a light heart, believing that he could soon throw off the few songs and interludes that seemed to be required. But he soon became engrossed in the problems set him by the dramatist, and devoted much of the autumn and winter of 1874–5 to the composition of *Peer Gynt*. The possibility of completing *Olav Trygvason* had receded, Ibsen had offered him generous terms, and the Norwegian Government had awarded him a stipend that allowed him liberty to live away from Christiania and give all his time to composition. He could no longer spend his holidays at Landaas, for the family estate had been sold, but a friend lent him a summer house or pavilion at Sandviken, and there he worked steadily at *Peer Gynt*. The score was finished at Fredensborg, in Denmark. The first presentation of *Peer Gynt* on the stage, with Grieg's music, took place on the 28th February 1876. The now familiar orchestral suites extracted from the two dozen pieces of incidental music achieved a still wider success and became the most popular of all his orchestral works.

In recent years voices (mainly those of dramatic producers) have been raised in criticism of the suitability of Grieg's *Peer Gynt* music for a drama so complex in its characterisation and symbolism. It is urged that several of Grieg's interludes are not only superfluous, having been originally conceived to fill in gaps during the cumbersome and lengthy scene-shifting operations of the nineteenth-century stage, but also distort the true nature of Ibsen's characters and situations. For

example, the beautiful little piece known as
Morning or *Morning Mood* and included in the first
orchestral suite has no dramatic or psychological
relevance to the fourth act of the play, before
which it occurs. Again, "Anitra's Dance", delightful
though it is, has given the average theatre-goer as
well as the average concert-goer a very different
picture of Anitra from the one Ibsen drew. Even
the music for muted strings that accompanies the
scene where Peer makes believe to drive his
mother to Soria Moria Castle, and finds at the end
of the fantastic journey that Aase's spirit has
indeed taken flight, has been regarded askance, for
all its reticence; while "Solveig's Song" has been
adversely criticised as too artificial, even operatic,
for the function it ought to serve in the drama.
The recent production of *Peer Gynt*, translated
into New Norse, at the National Theatre in Oslo
has aimed at removing what the producer con-
siders to be accretions of romantic material,
including the music of Grieg, and allowing Ibsen's
work to make its full emotional impact. Music
there must be, however, since the playwright
specifically calls for it; and the contemporary composer Harald Saeverud has been commissioned
to write certain fragments—including, of course, a
setting of "Solveig's Song", in a deliberately de-
romanticised style. It may be that as far as the
stage is concerned Grieg's *Peer Gynt* music has had
its day, and will in the future lead an entirely
independent existence in the two familiar orchestral suites. On the other hand, Grieg's critics
sometimes overlook the fact that the Suites do not
contain by any means the whole of his *Peer Gynt*

music, nor, speaking generally, the ones that are dramatically the most effective. The music to Act I, with its imitations of the Hardanger fiddle at the wedding, playing the traditional *halling* and *springdans*, could hardly be bettered, and there is a brief, little-known Prelude to Act III, scored for strings and horns, that foreshadows Sibelius. Again, it is only fair to Grieg to recall that, like many another composer for the stage, he was worried by the author with detailed instructions on how the music should be planned and even what it should sound like. Ibsen himself admitted that it was Grieg's score that had done more than anything else to make the public swallow the bitter medicine he had concocted for it in *Peer Gynt*.

CHAPTER V

1875–1882

THE year 1875, which had begun so auspiciously for Grieg by linking his name with those of Norway's two greatest literary figures, ended on a note of sadness. Both his father and his mother died during the autumn months. His *Ballade* (op. 24) for piano, in the form of variations on a folk-tune from Valdres, was written at this period; its deep poignancy may be due partly to the emotions of personal grief, but the same tragic atmosphere is to be found in the settings of poems by Ibsen (op. 25) composed earlier in the year. Among them are some of the most perfect and economical of all his songs: "A Swan", "With a Water-lily", and "Departed". Hardly inferior are the five Paulsen songs (op. 26) written about the same time and including "With a Primrose" and "On the Woodland Path".

These songs, so closely related in spirit and style to Solveig's two songs in *Peer Gynt*, help to show how Grieg was being irresistibly drawn towards the heart of Norwegian folk-music. As far back as the summer of 1869, while on holiday at Landaas, he had come across for the first time Lindeman's collection of folk-tunes arranged for the piano and entitled *Aeldre og nyere Fjeldmelodier* ("Old and new

Mountain Melodies"). Lindeman was one of the most distinguished of an important family of musicians whose home was originally in Trondhjem. In 1840 he contributed a musical supplement to a book of folk-poetry edited by Jorgen Moe, and in the following year published a larger collection of tunes. In 1848 he was awarded a State grant to travel about the country and note down further discoveries. He found a wealth of material in the villages, farms, and saeters, and his main collection, published in three parts between 1853 and 1867, contains nearly six hundred tunes. The first-fruits of Grieg's enthusiastic study of this work were the *Norwegian Dances and Songs* (op. 17) for piano published in 1870 and comprising seventeen tunes from Lindeman, enriched with Grieg's original and pianistic harmonisations. From now onwards Grieg was to draw repeatedly upon Lindeman for the folk-tunes he worked into various compositions; only in the last phase of his career, the *Folk-Tunes* (op. 66) and the *Slaatter* (op. 72), both of which will be referred to later, did he go to other sources. His discovery of *Mountain Melodies* also influenced those songs and piano pieces that do not contain direct folk-song quotations: the *Pictures of Folk-Life* (op. 19), for example, finished at Landaas in 1871—a set of vivid piano sketches, the best known being the *Norwegian Bridal Procession*. It is interesting to note, by the way, that this picturesque subject had a special appeal to the Norwegian romantics; it was painted by the artist Tidemand, and described in Bjørnson's story *Brudeslaatten*, which was published two or three years after Grieg's op. 19.

A few months after the first production of *Peer Gynt* in August 1876, Grieg went to Bayreuth to attend the Wagner Festival. He sent home to the journal *Bergenposten* notices of the first performances of *The Ring* which show a sturdy independence of judgment. In spite of the prevailing Wagner fever he kept his head. He admired the vast design of *The Ring*, and respected Wagner's command of the orchestra, but did not conceal his antipathy to the luxuriance and restlessness of Wagner's mature style. One of his notices refers to "the numerous chromatic transitions, the ceaseless changes of harmony, which result in one's being gradually overcome by nervous irritability, and finally by complete apathy". Lack of emotional reserve seemed to him intolerable in art as in everyday life. "Whoever reads the older Eddas", he wrote to his American friend Finck, "will soon realise their wonderful power and conciseness of expression, their ability to say much in few words. . . . The same is true of the Norwegian Sagas of the Kings, especially those of Snorre Sturlason. The more deeply the heart is moved the more reserved and enigmatic is the expression. The language always remains dry, serious, and dignified. The stormy ocean of the passions is felt rather than glimpsed. This saga literature is the basis on which Bjørnson and Ibsen have built. It can be said that in a similar way folk-song represents in music the inner life of the people. What the poets have achieved in this respect is what I have always striven after, perhaps above all in my settings of the deeply felt poems of the peasant-poets Vinje and Garborg. The exuberant

richness of outward expression, so characteristic
of the German, is foreign to the nature of the
Norseman." These observations were written
towards the end of Grieg's life, but they can be
taken as representing his views at the period we
have been describing. They show how different
was the Scandinavian romantic temperament
from the German, and explain how it was that
Grieg always felt that Norwegian art had closer
bonds with France than with Germany. His
ingrained dislike of unbridled emotion—he complained bitterly of excesses of *rubato* in performances of his works—made it difficult for him, in
spite of his catholic tastes, to enjoy the later
German romantics, such as Richard Strauss and
Max Reger.

During the winter of 1877 Grieg spent some time
on a task for which he has been severely criticised.
This was the addition of parts for second piano to
certain of Mozart's Sonatas—those in F (K. 533),
C (K. 545), G (K. 283), and the Fantasia and
Sonata in C minor (K. 475 and K. 457). As
Grieg's additions entirely alter the harmonic
implications of the originals and destroy the
clarity of Mozart's keyboard texture it is difficult to
defend him against the charge of vandalism. Yet
there is no doubt that he took these liberties not
from self-conceit but out of sincere admiration
for a particular aspect of Mozart's genius. It was
Mozart's telling use of chromatics that so much
aroused Grieg's enthusiasm, and drove him to
commit the rash action of attempting to merge
Mozart's chromatic writing with his own. This
becomes clearer in the light of an article written

4

by Grieg in 1897: "Excepting Bach, who here, as
everywhere, is the fundamental pillar on which all
modern music rests, no one has understood as well
as Mozart how to use the chromatic scale to
express the highest effect in music. We must go as
far as Wagner before we find chromatic harmonies
used for the expression of ardent feeling (*Innigkeit*).
In the case of Spohr, who made extensive use of
them, and who in many respects followed Mozart,
they remain without any deep significance." Grieg
goes on to reveal special affection for Mozart's
chamber works, mentioning the G minor Quintet,
the Piano Quintet in E flat, the Piano Quartet in
G minor, and the introduction to the String
Quartet in C, with its "'bold chromatic effects,
which even liberal musicians of this time were
unable to digest". The D minor Piano Concerto
was another work after Grieg's own heart. He
believed that Mozart would not have found
Wagner altogether alien to his nature; in fact, he
would have been "as delighted as a child with all
the new acquisitions in the development of drama
and orchestra".

The Griegs spent the summer and winter of
1877 in the romantic Hardanger district of
western Norway, first on a farm at Upper Børve
and later at Lofthus. Their hosts were a peasant
couple, Hans and Brita Utne, whose devotion to
their regional costume and lore was a perpetual
delight to the town-bred visitors. Edvard, who
could only compose contentedly in complete soli-
tude, had a hut built near the house to hold his
piano and writing table. As there were still inter-
ruptions from passers-by who stopped to listen to

the composer at work, Grieg got the help of the peasants in moving the structure bodily down to the edge of the fjord, to a sheltered spot commanding a view of the Folgefond glacier.

At Lofthus was written the earliest of the songs to poems by A. O. Vinje ("Along the River"), a setting for baritone solo, horns, and strings of an eerie old Norse Ballad, *Den Bergtekne* ("The Mountain Thrall") (op. 32), and the *Album of Songs for Male Voices* (op. 30). Lindeman's *Mountain Melodies* were again the source of the twelve folk-tunes freely arranged for male voices in various groupings, and ranging from the boisterous or jocular to the intense devotion of traditional chorale in "The Great White Host". Altogether this is one of the freshest and most endearing of all Grieg's vocal works. The two *Improvisations on Norwegian Folk-Tunes* for piano (op. 29) are less spontaneous; as the composer said they were written to order—to swell the fund for the creation of a memorial to Holberg—and bear all the marks of it. At Lofthus also he worked on his first String Quartet, in G Minor (op. 27), which uses as a "motto-theme" the opening phrase of the first of the Ibsen songs, "Minstrels", op. 25, no. 1. There is a good deal of internal evidence to show that this Quartet strongly influenced Debussy in composing his Quartet, also in G minor; if so, the child has proved more successful than the parent. Grieg was always unlucky in his handling of the string quartet; his earliest effort, produced to order in his student days, he destroyed or lost; another work begun in 1891 was never completed, and the G minor Quartet suffers not only from monotony of texture but also from an excess of mannerisms that makes it resemble a parody on the composer's style. It is probable that Grieg was too much preoccupied at this period with folk-tune on the one hand, and his harmonic discoveries on the other, to write in what is nowadays generally called the "linear" manner that a good quartet demands. His ingenuous attitude towards structural problems comes out in a letter to Frants Beyer, written in 1884, where he refers to this quartet *à propos* of the tendency of inattentive audiences to burst in with applause during a pause in the first movement: "You know that in my bigger works I have the habit, weakness, or call it what you will, of breaking off, for the sake of structural effect and thematic contrast, in the principal key before the second theme enters, instead of following the general practice of making a transition to lead imperceptibly into the latter. I do the same thing again after the return of the first subject in the recapitulation."

With the years 1878 and 1879 comes a noticeable gap in Grieg's creative life. He attributed it himself to chronic ill health, although it is difficult to reconcile such an explanation with his vast and energetic programmes of concert tours in Germany and other lands at this period. The real reason, one suspects, is that his talent, always a delicate and fitful one, had become inhibited both by the individual character of the musical idiom he had developed within the past ten years, and by the increasing rigour of his self-criticism. And it is certain that his mounting fame, the many demands made on him by publishers and concert promoters, and the widening circle of his friendships and correspondence, took heavy toll of his time and nervous resources. An abortive attempt to write a Trio in C minor for violin, cello, and piano is indicated by the survival in manuscript of an andante movement for this combination, dated 1878.

Not until the spring of 1880 did he resume his composition of the Vinje songs (op. 33) that had engaged his interest at Lofthus. In these songs he set for the first time words in the Landsmaal or New Norse, a form of Norwegian based on the peasant dialects, which a number of writers were advocating as an alternative to the Dano-Norwegian or Riksmaal in general use among educated people. A. O. Vinje, a poet and prose writer of peasant origin, adopted Landsmaal in a somewhat modified form; he drew inspiration from the land of Norway in all its sternness and beauty, and from the lives of the people who lived closest to the land. Grieg published his Vinje settings in two books, each containing six songs. Most widely known are "Vaaren" ("The Spring") and "Den Saarede" ("The Wounded One"), for the composer made an arrangement of these for string orchestra under the title of *Elegiac Melodies* op. 34). In "Gamle Mor" ("Old Mother"), which was written several years before the rest, we recognise a son's grateful tribute to Gesine Grieg.

The poignant words of "Vaaren" must have been much in Grieg's mind later in the same year in which he had made his setting of them. Among his friends there was one for whom spring would never come again, who would never again see the unpent waters cascading from the snowfields. On the 23rd August Grieg, with Bjørnson and thousands of the citizens of Bergen, followed in the funeral procession of Ole Bull. In the name of Norwegian music he laid on the coffin a laurel wreath, and a few days later conducted the only composition of Bull's that has survived its author, the melody *Saeterjentens Søndag* ("The Herdgirl's Sunday") and his own *Last Spring*. The kinship of the two melodies must have struck many hearers.

In the autumn of 1880 Grieg was induced to become conductor of the Bergen Harmonic Society. He held the post for two seasons, and although conducting was never a strong interest with him he worked hard to raise the standard of the orchestra, and to familiarise the musical public of Bergen with important works like Schubert's C major Symphony and Mozart's Requiem. This was the last time he was to accept a public appointment. In 1881 he suggested half in jest to Dr. Abraham, then head of the Leipzig publishing firm of Peters, that he should be given a contract with a fixed annual payment in return for writing works commissioned by the firm, as well as for assigning to them the copyright of whatever he chose to offer them for publication. Abraham took him at his word. A few years later Peters bought up all rights of other publishers, whether Danish or German, in Grieg's earlier works.

This arrangement, while giving Grieg complete security from business cares, and ensuring that his works, in their familiar pink covers, reached every music-shop in Europe, had certain drawbacks from the artistic standpoint. It led to the use of

German titles instead of Norwegian ones even when the works were performed in English-speaking countries, and what was worse, to the association of many of Grieg's songs with faulty German translations. Outside Scandinavian countries few singers can be found who are willing to learn Danish and the two forms of Norwegian well enough to sing most of Grieg's songs in the original; but the art of translation is so much better understood nowadays that there is no longer any excuse for perpetuating the ineptitudes of some of the published German versions.

On the strength of his newly found independence Grieg was able to resign his appointment at Bergen, refuse an offer from Helsingfors of the directorship of the Conservatory there, and after spending part of the summer at Carlsbad to return to Bergen and concentrate on his writing.

CHAPTER VI

1882–1892

THE firm of Peters were soon pressing Grieg to try to repeat some of his more successful achievements of earlier years. It was the heyday of the piano, not only as the chosen instrument of the lionised virtuoso, but also as the humble household orchestra, and a new volume of piano pieces by Edvard Grieg was always received with jubilation in Leipzig. At the beginning of 1883 we find Grieg at work on a second Piano Concerto that never advanced beyond the sketch-book stage, and completing a second set of the *Lyric Pieces* that had come as a boon to the amateur sixteen years before. For duet-players he followed the *Norwegian Dances* (op. 35), which were arrangements of tunes from Lindeman, with the *Valses caprices* (op. 37), two pieces showing the composer's ability to write with distinction in the conventional salon forms of his time. A weightier work was the Sonata for cello and piano (op. 36), dedicated to the composer's brother John who also had received a professional training at Leipzig but had chosen to follow an administrative career with cello-playing as a relaxation. Although this Sonata shows the same uncertainty of structure as Grieg's other works of the kind it is fluent and effective,

particularly in the second movement, which recalls,
not only in melodic outline but also in the use
of the cello, the "Homage March" from *Sigurd*.

Grieg's often-avowed love for retirement and
domesticity was oddly combined with an insatiable
appetite for international fame. Ambitious and
invariably successful concert tours carried him
about Germany, Holland, France and Italy with
the enviable freedom travellers enjoyed in those
halcyon 1880's. In Holland the Griegs stayed
over Christmas, 1883, as the guests of Julius Röntgen, Edvard thoroughly enjoying the Dutch
museums, sand-dunes, and oysters, and in the
following year Röntgen returned the visit and
spent a week at Lofthus. Thus a friendship was
formed that is recorded in Röntgen's memoirs of
Grieg and his music.[1] Grieg made friends readily,
even among fellow-musicians, for his talent was
individual enough to stimulate interest but special-
ised enough to protect him from jealousy. Nina
was often his companion on these tours, and shared
with him the triumphs of the concert platform. In
Rome she brought tears to the eyes of the mis-
anthropic Ibsen by singing to him "A Swan" and
other settings of his poems.

But the cosmopolitan background of his working
life only threw into relief Grieg's affection for his
own country. He had now been for many years
the musical spokesman of Norway, and it was to
him that the sponsors of the Holberg Festival, held
in Bergen in 1884 to celebrate the two hundredth
anniversary of the birth of that great comic playwright, turned when they sought an appropriate

[1] See Bibliography.

tribute. Grieg responded with a cantata for male voices and a suite of pieces, originally written for piano, in the dance-forms popular in Holberg's day. Holberg was influenced by French models in his comedies of Scandinavian manners in the eighteenth century, and has been called the Molière of the North. Grieg's success in reproducing the atmosphere of the period and in imitating the style of the French *clavécinistes* makes *From Holberg's Time* one of the best, as it is one of the earliest, modern examples of pastiche.

This same summer Grieg strengthened his personal ties with western Norway by beginning to build the villa Troldhaugen ("The Hill of the Trolls") near Bergen, which was to be his headquarters for the rest of his life and a museum consecrated to his memory after death. The Westland mountains attracted him more and more. Each year, in the height of summer, he would make a tour among their moors and glaciers, generally in company with his neighbour and friend Frants Beyer, sometimes also with a visitor from abroad. Among those who were to share these expeditions in Grieg's later years were Percy Grainger and Frederick Delius. It was even hoped that Brahms would some day come to Norway, but this was not to be. Grieg's passion for the natural beauty of the country is constantly coming out in his letters; for example, he wrote to Beyer from Copenhagen on the 26th April 1886: "What would you say to a quiet morning in the boat between skerry and cliffs? The other day I felt so full of longing for it that it grew into a calm Song of Gratitude . . ." Here he gives a sketch of the little piece later called

"Tak" ("Thanks") in Book 7 of the *Lyric Pieces*
(op. 62, no. 2). In the same way, some five years
later when he is in a mood of despondency and feels
no longer young he cries: "To the mountains!
To the mountains! Only there is healing!" In
1886 he had as companion the Danish poet Holger
Drachmann; they had agreed to collaborate in an
album of songs recording their impressions of the
mountains, and eventually produced *Memories of
Travel from Mountain and Fjord* (op. 44). Unfortunately the quality of the songs does not come up
to the expectations aroused by such a title.

Grieg's first visit to England[1] took place in
April, 1888. He followed Tchaikovsky as guest
conductor of the Philharmonic Society, and on the
3rd May took part in a programme at St. James's
Hall that is interesting for more than one reason.
It included not only Grieg's *Elegiac Melodies*
conducted by the composer, the Piano Concerto
with Grieg as soloist, and a group of his songs sung
by Carlotta Elliott, but also the first performance
in England of Bizet's *Jeux d'Enfants*, conducted by
Frederick Cowen. In a chamber recital a fortnight
later the artists were Edvard and Nina Grieg and
Fru Norman-Neruda. The instrumental items
included the F major Violin Sonata (op. 8) and
part of the C minor Violin Sonata (op. 45), and
some of the Norwegian Folk Songs and Dances for
piano (op. 17). In August Grieg came again to
England to conduct at the Birmingham Festival
his early Overture *In Autumn*, which he had revised
and rescored for the occasion, and the *Holberg*
Suite. On yet another London visit, in the spring

[1] As an artist that is; he is said to have accompanied his parents on a visit
n his boyhood.

of 1889, he played all three of the Violin Sonatas with three celebrated violinists who happened to be in the country: Lady Hallé, Joachim and Johannes Wolf.

From this period dates the beginning of Grieg's friendship with Frederick Delius, an event that was to determine the direction of Delius's career and introduce important elements into his musical style. Delius had already, since first visiting Norway in 1881 as an agent in his father's woollen business, made several trips to the country, had learnt to speak the language, and had become acquainted with Ibsen and other leading figures in drama and music. In 1887 he met Grieg in Leipzig, where it is said that Grieg organised a Christmas festivity at which Halvorsen, Sinding, and Delius were each to present a new work; but the convivial side of the evening triumphed over its artistic purpose. Grieg was so strongly impressed with Delius's gifts that he consented to plead with Julius Delius, of Bradford, to allow his son to abandon orange-planting and wool-peddling for a musician's career.

Arriving home in 1889 after more concerts in Paris and Brussels Grieg completed the scoring of the early scenes of his ill-fated opera, *Olav Trygvason*, arranging them for concert performance, and ending the estrangement between Bjørnson and himself by dedicating the work, in this form, to his defaulting librettist. Even after this lapse of time he seems to have hoped that Bjørnson might change his mind and finish the text. In a letter addressed from Paris on the 26th December 1889 he begs his friend Beyer to act as intermediary.

"He will understand you and sympathise both with you and me if you ask him to continue *Olav Trygvason*. He is now trying to get me to set to music *The King Comes*, a piece he is engaged on, but I have told him it is not for me . . . I want *Olav Trygvason* or some Norwegian tale."

Grieg's creative powers were again at a low ebb. He had written little during the past four or five years. Like so many composers of limited range who have the fortune to capture the popular ear, he was continually kept busy with arrangements and rearrangements of earlier works, and with giving performances in which he figured as a celebrity. His health, uncertain since his student days, now began to cause him serious trouble. In proportion as his reputation grew among the undiscerning, he became more dissatisfied than ever with everything he wrote. After finishing the third of his Violin Sonatas he abandoned all attempt to compose in the more extended forms of instrumental music. It seemed as though he could no longer write spontaneously except under the stimulus of Norwegian scenery, poetry, or folk-tune. Inspiration of this kind came to him fairly often during the early 'nineties. The Romance for Two Pianos, or *Old Norse Melody with Variations* (op. 51) —a work later arranged for orchestra—is founded on a song called "Sigurd and the Troll-bride" which had been included in *Six Norwegian Mountain Melodies*, a collection of piano transcriptions made a considerable time before. He came into touch with folk-music at first hand in the summer of 1893, when a holiday in the Jotunheim mountains with Beyer enabled him to take down some

fine melodies from the singing of the peasants.
Some of these tunes were arranged for piano as
Norwegian Folk-Tunes (op. 66), a collection of interest not only for its own sake—one feels that Grieg
was carried away by the loveliness of the melodies
and surpassed himself in originality of treatment—
but also because one number, "I Ola-dalom,
i Ola-Kjönn" gave Delius a theme, and some
harmonic ideas, for his orchestral piece *On Hearing
the First Cuckoo in Spring*.

Röntgen gives a lively account of a holiday tour
in 1893 that led to the collection of a number of
folk-tunes. The following is an extract:

> Grieg and I travelled from Lofthus by *stolkjärre*
> (a small carriage on two wheels, to hold three
> people) to the Sognefjord, whence we reached
> Skjolden by rowing boat. From there the road
> leads uphill to Turtegrø. On the way we picked up
> a *spillemaend*, that is a player on the Hardanger
> fiddle, and he gave us his tunes during the whole
> of the glorious drive. How well the music suited the
> surroundings! Grieg listened rapt, his head nod-
> ding in time to the music, and in his hand a glass of
> wine which he kept offering to the player. "This is
> Norway," he cried, with gleaming eyes.
>
> It was a warm August afternoon, the fjord lay
> dark green and we, stretched out on sacks of hay,
> let the splendid mountain landscape slip slowly
> past our eyes like a tapestry. We made the journey
> up to Turtegrø on horseback, but before we started
> Grieg drank with me in token of brotherhood. . . .
> The Jotunheim range now appeared gradually
> before our eyes: Fanaraak, Ringstindene, and
> finally the great Skagastølstind, the Matterhorn of
> Norway. The dark rock was tinted reddish-brown

by the evening sun. At last we reached the hut of
Ole Berge, the well-known guide, and received a
hearty welcome from him.

Suddenly we heard from outside the yodel that
was Frants Beyer's signal, and presently he was
with us in radiant Jotunheim mood.

Beside Ole Berge's hut were two more hillside
huts where the *jenter* (saeter-girls) lived. Of course
we made our way to these two on the first evening,
and Frants Beyer persuaded the girls, after some
hesitation, to sing.

For the first time I heard Norwegian folk-songs
in their proper surroundings; what a fine effect they
had there! Frants Beyer told us how in the morning, when the cows were being milked, while the
girls sang, he laid his music-paper on the cow's back
and so had got his songs "fresh from the cow".

Early the next morning I heard Ole Berge's sister
calling the goats and singing. There was singing
everywhere! Among Grieg's posthumous manu-
scripts I found a sheet dated: Turtegrø 1893, with
various motives from the Jotunheim. [Here half a
dozen folk tunes are quoted] . . .

After some days we journeyed from Turtegrø
over the Kaiser Pass to Skogadalsbøen, a tourist
hut, the central point of the Jotunheim. We had
pig veir (peak weather) for the whole of our trip;
Grieg walked or rode on horse-back, Beyer sang
with me as we went along snatches of the String
Quartets of Mozart and enjoyed the music just as
much as if he was hearing a most finished performance of it. By the Gjertvasbre, a gigantic glacier in
circular formation, we rested a little. The glacier
gleamed purest white. It was a great moment.
Those who had never seen Grieg in the high
mountains on an occasion like this could not know
him as he really was; only then did his genial

nature, free from all bodily encumbrance, find its full expression.

Skogadalsbø is, as I have said, the centre of the Jotunheim. From it passes and dales lead in every direction. This tourist hut is the best situated, and the most comfortable in the whole of the Jotunheim. It lies on a spur of the mountain from which one looks down far into the wooded Skogadal, with its rushing *elv* (mountain stream), a striking contrast to the otherwise treeless Jotunheim. In Skogadalsbø we had an unforgettable evening. At that time the tourist hut was in charge of Tollef and Brit Holmestad. The wife had recently had a child and her sister, Gjendine Slaalien, was staying with her to help her. This Gjendine, born near the Gjendin lake, had been named after it by her parents. She was the only person in the whole of Norway with this name. When first we saw her she was rocking her sister's child in her arms, singing it to sleep with the following song: [Here Röntgen gives the melody of "Gjendine's Lullaby", arranged by Grieg for the piano as op. 66, no. 19]. . . . Gjendine could also play on the goat-horn, an instrument on which only the first three notes of the minor scale can be sounded. With these three notes she could produce the most original melodies.

So passed the evening in this pleasant hut with song and gaiety, and when we came out there lay the mountains in the fantastic light of the moon while from the depths sounded the rushing of the stream. Gjendine stood on a rock and sang us the lullaby again. How overwhelmingly beautiful it all was! Grieg said to me: "You are certainly lucky; one doesn't hear this kind of thing very often in Norway nowadays!"

The following morning we left Skogadalsbø. When we had already gone some distance along our

way we heard the notes of the goat-horn. Gjendine
was bidding us farewell by playing the following
tune, which became ever softer and died away in
long notes: [Röntgen again quotes the melody].

Grieg's Lyric Piece, entitled "Heimweh" ("Longing for Home" (op. 57, no. 6)) makes use of this
same motive of three notes.

The sound of pastoral music is also suggested in
"Shepherd Boy", the first of the fifth book of *Lyric
Pieces*, which was completed in 1891. This is one of
the best of the sets, containing besides "Shepherd
Boy" a "Gangar" (Norwegian dance in march
style), a "March of the Dwarfs", and the remark-
able "advanced" impressionistic piece called
"Bell-ringing".

The harmonisation of op. 66 was completed
during another mountain-tour, again with Röntgen and Beyer. Grieg described the harmonies as
"hair-raising", but defended them on the ground
that they were born in the brain, not at the keyboard; but that with the Væringfoss at one's feet
one becomes more daring than in the valleys.

In the autumn of 1891 Grieg's friends and
admirers celebrated in Christiania the twenty-fifth
anniversary of his first public concert in the
Norwegian capital. The events included a choral
and orchestral concert, a banquet at which Ibsen
was one of the principal speakers, and a torchlight
procession arranged by the university students.

What Johansen, the Norwegian biographer of
Grieg, terms "the monotonous 'nineties" now
began to pass by; there is much to chronicle of
Grieg's life as international artist and public figure,
unhappily little to record of his activity as

composer. That he had not finally abandoned his early ambitions to write in the traditional forms of instrumental music is proved by the existence of two movements of a second String Quartet, begun at Copenhagen in the winter of 1891–2. He still kept before him also the idea of writing an opera on some national theme. A letter dated the 19th June 1893 mentions a visit from Ibsen, and the poet's proposal to adapt as an opera-text his historical drama, *The Warriors at Helgeland*. In an earlier letter (27th August 1883) Grieg had written appreciatively of Wagner's *Tristan* and *Parsifal* and wistfully of his own fading ambitions: "Now you will realise", he says, "why so often I go and gaze up at the clouds, as if I could find there the Norwegian drama in Norwegian music that I have dreamt of, that I have always believed I should write one day, though I am now beginning to think that Fate has decreed it shall be the work of another." An attempt to compose an oratorio with Bjørnson came to nothing, though Bjørnson on this occasion carried out his side of the plan and completed the text. Grieg had chosen the subject —*Peace*—after reading a speech by Bjørnson to the Workers' Association, and feeling that it accorded with his own cherished desire to write a requiem for modern times "without dogma". It has been suggested that the realism of Bjørnson's poem, with its references to factories, banks, and the electric telegraph proved too much for Grieg's romantic temperament.

On the 11th June 1892 Edvard and Nina celebrated their silver wedding at Troldhaugen. It was one of those festivities, partly domestic, partly public, that the Scandinavian peoples carry off so naturally and so charmingly. The number and variety of gifts and messages of congratulation that arrived from all over the world were a measure of the popularity the Griegs had gained in the course of their visits to many lands. In the evening they entertained to supper a hundred and thirty guests—mainly neighbours and fellow-citizens of Bergen—and the more general festivities included firework displays, boating parties on the fjord, and choral singing.

The following year Grieg was made an honorary D.Mus. of Cambridge University. His fellow-recipients of this distinction were Boito, Bruch, Saint-Saëns, and Tchaikovsky—altogether a very odd team, one would have thought, to pick for academic honours. Something has already been said about Grieg's cordial relations with other eminent composers. In Tchaikovsky, whom he first met in Leipzig in 1888, he found much to admire; and Tchaikovsky has left us one of the best descriptions of Grieg as he appeared in middle life: "Into the room came a very little, middle-aged man, very thin and with shoulders of unequal height. His fair hair was brushed back high and he had a thin, almost youthful-looking beard, and side whiskers. . . . He had uncommonly attractive blue eyes of medium size, irresistibly fascinating, like the gaze of an innocent, noble child." Grieg's charm was even powerful enough to penetrate the barrier of rudeness that Brahms built up round himself. They met first in Leipzig in 1885, at the house of Brahms's friends, Heinrich and Elisabeth von Herzogenberg. On this occasion

Grieg played his *Norwegian Bridal Procession* (op. 19, no. 2) and Brahms his G minor Ballade. Ten years later, in Vienna, they saw more of each other and Grieg and Röntgen lunched with Brahms at the famous "Red Hedgehog". Not unnaturally, Brahms singled out for special praise Grieg's *Ballade* (op. 24)—a work in which there is more than a suggestion of Brahms's own manner. Grieg, on his side, expressed admiration for the *German Requiem* and Brahms's songs and chamber music. Contemporary French music always interested him. When he heard Franck's *Les Béatitudes* in Leipzig in 1895 he wrote to Matthison-Hansen: "In my opinion, no living composer can compare with him." He revelled in the score of Carmen, at one time thought of taking lessons in orchestration from Edouard Lalo, and almost at the close of his life was thrilled at hearing Debussy's *L'Après-midi d'un faune* at its first performance in Christiania in 1906. To him it seemed a perfect and wholly desirable antithesis to what he called "the German plum-pudding"—his favourite term of disparagement for the works of Max Reger. Unhappily his admiration for Debussy was not fully reciprocated. After Grieg's concert in Paris in April, 1903, Debussy wrote acidly about the Piano Concerto in his column in *Gil Blas*: "Je n'ai jamais compris pourquoi il était traversé çà et là par des sonneries de trompettes guerrières annonçant généralement qu'un petit cantabile où l'on se pâme va commencer."

In an obituary article on Verdi, which appeared in English in *The Nineteenth Century* for March 1901, Grieg said that he had always been an admirer of

the Italian composer, although "at the Leipzig
Conservatory in the 'fifties and 'sixties a mention of
Verdi was met with nothing but a contemptuous
shrug of the shoulders and the smile of superiority".
He tells of a curious incident that occurred at the
Theatre Royal, Copenhagen, when *Otello* was
being performed under Svendsen (probably in
1898). When the orchestra began to play the prelude to the last act (he means the introduction to
Desdemona's "Willow Song") he felt eyes being
turned towards him; the melody here happening
to follow the familiar Grieg progression (lah, se,
me), was inevitably regarded as having been
composed under his influence.[1]

[1] Verdi's phrase may even have recalled specifically the opening of *Gutten*,
the first of the Vinje songs (op. 33).

CHAPTER VII

1892–1901

WE have seen that after publishing the Third Violin Sonata (op. 45) Grieg completed nothing else in the larger forms of music; he had realised that he did not possess the intellectual equipment required for organising such a work as a sonata or quartet, and making it into a convincing structure. Any success he had achieved in this field must be attributed to the freshness and beauty he had been able to give to the separate parts and details of a composition, rather than to the sweep and cohesion of the whole. His talent was for the lyrical, richly coloured miniature, for a highly individual turn of melody, for harmonic originality, for finding a musical expression for some mood "recollected in tranquillity" or experienced through the work of another artist in another medium, especially poetry.

It is a sign of Grieg's integrity and sensitiveness that he recognised and faced his limitations before it was too late. With less of those qualities, and more obtuseness and vanity, he might have turned into another Gade, writing moribund symphonies and concertos far into a respectable old age. Instead, from about his fiftieth year he produced a small but distinguished quantity of songs, piano pieces, and folk-music arrangements.

In making a rapid survey of Grieg's later songs
we may begin with the *Six Poems* (in Danish) of
Holger Drachmann (op. 49) which Grieg set in
1889, three years after his first collaboration with
Drachmann in the travel-songs, *From Mountain
and Fjord*. Grieg always responds to a finely drawn
picture of natural beauty, and the *Six Poems*
include some first-rate examples: "Rock, O wave",
"Now is the evening light and long", "Christmas
Snow", and "Spring Rain". The whole set illustrates the effectiveness of Grieg's piano accompaniments, which are so often full of detailed and
excellent writing but never assert themselves
unduly over the voice-parts. Another set of *Six
Songs* (op. 48), also written in 1889, has texts by
various German poets, and includes some admir-
able songs. Despite the choice of German poems
by Heine, Geibel, Uhland and others Grieg's
setting are remarkably Norwegian in colouring.
This is true especially of No. 4 ("Verschwiegene
Nachtigall") where he matches the mediaeval
imagery of Walther von der Vogelweide with
melodic phrases of archaic pattern.

In 1894 Grieg returned to song-writing in his
own language with two books of settings of verses
by Paulsen—*Norway* (op. 58) and *Elegiac Poems*
(op. 59). Here poet and musician join in affec-
tionate tribute to their native country; the English
listener must try to put himself into their place to
share the quiet, intimate rapture and melancholy
of their moods. Another minor Norwegian poet,
Vilhelm Krag, gave Grieg the texts for *Five Songs*
(op. 60), among which occur some charmingly
homely genre pictures of peasant life: "Little

Kirsten", with its picturesque suggestions of
cuckoo and spinning wheel, "The Mother Sings",
"And I will have a Sweetheart"—an evocation of
the ritual of the old midsummer fire-dances—and
a striking song, "There cried a bird", where Grieg
makes use of a phrase imitated from the cry of a
gull heard over the Hardanger Fjord. The *Children's Songs* (op. 61), sung for the first time in public
by Nina at a concert in Copenhagen in the spring
of 1895, are settings of verses of the nursery rhyme
type from a children's reading book edited by
Nordahl Rolfsen; they are without question among
the aptest songs ever composed for children.
"Dobbin's Good-night Song" (no. 5), has become
popular in an English version. The composer's
own favourite was "The Sea" (no. 1); "I think it
is the freshest", he wrote, "and has the most character. There is a C sharp that must sound like sea-
salt." All the other songs present facets of Norwegian life: the Christmas tree (no. 2), the herd-
boy's call (no. 3), the fisherman's song (no. 4), the
mountains (no. 6); and the collection is rounded
off with a Hymn of the Fatherland (no. 7).

The *Children's Songs* were finished at the beginning of 1895. Soon afterwards Grieg began a cycle
of songs that stand by themselves in their intense
feeling and cumulative power. His interest in the
Landsmaal movement that had been aroused when
he set Vinje's poems was again quickened by a
reading of Arne Garborg's *Haugtussa*, a story—told
in a series of lyric poems—of a young girl,
Veslemøy, lured by the enchantments of the troll-
haunted mounds of Norwegian folk-tale. Grieg
found himself writing at white heat—as he told

Röntgen, "The music is already composed by the poet; one only has to write it down." When the cycle was published in 1898 it contained eight songs; others remain in manuscript. In spite of their great beauty the *Haugtussa* songs have never reached a wide public, for they must be sung in the original Landsmaal to make their full effect of pathos and magic. It is much to be deplored that the gramophone records of the whole cycle made by Kirsten Flagstad are no longer obtainable. Like the majority of Grieg's songs they are all in strophic form, which the ballad-like character of Garborg's verse justifies. Within this simple framework there is rich variety of melodic line, rhythm, harmony, and keyboard effect. The phrasing and declamation of the voice-part are particularly sensitive. "Declamation", wrote Nina Grieg in a letter to the Swiss Pastor L. Monastier-Schroeder after the composer's death, "was always his strongest point. If only you knew how splendidly his Norwegian songs are declaimed! Unfortunately it is almost entirely lost in translation. I am sorry to say that I have not the least influence with Peters. It is in vain that I have suggested various people to translate the posthumous songs. The publisher has always 'chosen someone else' and he has not even sent me the translations for revision." The *Haugtussa* songs are certainly enough to break the heart of any conscientious translator, though one of them, "Kidlings' Dance", has been fairly often sung in German.

Grieg seems to have closed his career as a song-writer seven years before his death. In 1900 he produced two books of settings of words by the

Danish poet Otto Benzon (op. 69 and op. 70).
Although these contain some fine songs—such as
"There rocks a boat on the waves" (op. 69, no. 1)
and "Radiant Night" (op. 70, no. 3)—they cannot
be compared with the poignant simplicity of the
best of the Norwegian songs.

It is a curious feature of his musical personality
that Grieg, even in some of his most mature works,
keeps the Danish and Norwegian backgrounds of
his experience quite distinct. This is nowhere
more clearly noticeable than in the *Lyric Pieces* for
piano, of which he published the last five sets
between 1893 and 1901. Some of these pieces,
such as "Home-sickness" (Book 6, op. 57, no. 6)
and "Tak" (Book 7, op. 62, no. 2), we have
already referred to as having been written under
the stimulus of the Norwegian scene. In keeping
with these are most of the pieces in Book 8
(op. 65), which includes "Wedding-day at Troldhaugen", several in Book 9 (op. 68) including
two—"Evening in the Mountains" and "Cradle
Song"—that the composer arranged for orchestra,
and again most of the tenth and final set (op. 71)
which is particularly rich in impressionistic writing
(as in no. 4, "Peace of the Woods") that reminds
us of Debussy. On the other hand, the drawing-
room elegance of "She dances" (op. 57, no. 5),
"Salon" (op. 65, no. 4) and "Grandmother's
Minuet" (op. 68, no. 2) belong to the kindly, comfortable, stylised world of the *Holberg* Suite—or, for
that matter, of "Anitra's Dance" in *Peer Gynt*: a
world as far removed from nature and folk-lore
as the Tivoli pleasure gardens from the Jotunheim.

It is worth emphasising at this point that as

Grieg grew older he showed no trace of artistic chauvinism or parochialism. On the contrary, he followed Ibsen in his contempt of those among his countrymen who believed in cutting themselves off from the cultural influences of the rest of Europe and becoming, in the language of *Peer Gynt*, "to themselves enough". The German critics who complained that Grieg failed to reach greater heights because he "stuck in a fjord" were lacking in perception. Like most of the greatest Norwegians of modern times, he was a widely travelled and widely read man, loving his own land passionately, but aware none the less of the dangers of cultural in-breeding. His breadth of vision was shown in his handling of the first Norwegian Music Festival, which was held at Bergen in the summer of 1898. National music was of course liberally represented in the programmes, but Grieg insisted, in the teeth of less liberally minded patriots, on inviting a first-class orchestra to come from abroad and set a standard for the Festival. His choice was the Amsterdam Concertgebouw Orchestra, under Mengelberg; its playing was a revelation to the Norwegians, and the artistic success of the Festival brought Grieg much satisfaction.

In the following year another landmark in the artistic history of the country was set up with the opening of the National Theatre in Christiania. Grieg's reconciliation with Bjørnson was now happily complete. He conducted the music to *Sigurd Jorsalfar* in the theatre, and stayed with the Bjørnsons in their ample and hospitable country house at Aulestad. This visit was to have an

unforeseen consequence. The newspapers at the
time were full of the Dreyfus case, and Grieg felt
so strongly about what he considered the unjust
action of the French Government that he wrote
there and then to Colonne, the promoter of the
Châtelet Theatre concerts, who had invited Grieg
to conduct a programme of his own works, and
declared that he could no longer bring himself to
appear before the French public. The letter was
passed round the Bjørnson household before being
sent off, and Bjørnson's son-in-law, Albert Langen,
persuaded Grieg to let him publish it in the
German press. A political gesture on the part of
an artist is always, in the full journalistic sense,
news, and Grieg soon found his letter being quoted
and discussed in the papers of more than one
country, including those of France, which naturally gave it a hostile reception. There was a sequel
three years later, when Grieg thought himself
justified in accepting a renewed invitation to conduct in Paris. *L'affaire Dreyfus* had by that time
died down, but his letter had not been forgotten,
and as he mounted the platform he was received
with catcalls, doubtless from an organised faction.
But he boldly went ahead with his programme, the
interruptors were thrown out, and the public
applauded. To their amusement Edvard and
Nina were escorted from the theatre after the
concert by a triple force of police. The programme
on this occasion included the Overture *In Autumn*,
the first *Peer Gynt* Suite, the first performance in
France of the early cantata *At a Southern Convent's
Gate*, the *Elegiac Melodies* for strings, and the
inevitable Piano Concerto with Raoul Pugno as

soloist. Only once before had Grieg gone out of his way to assert his political convictions, and then it was with less spectacular results. During the controversy with Sweden over the union of the kingdoms he had at first felt it his duty to refuse to conduct in Stockholm, but two years later, in 1896, he had relented and was made to realise the warmth of sympathy that existed between the two peoples in spite of constitutional difficulties. Nevertheless, the achievement of complete Norwegian independence in 1905 filled him with pride and thankfulness.

CHAPTER VIII

1901–1907

THE last six years of Grieg's life were heavy with physical suffering and mental lassitude. The old pulmonary trouble, dating from his student days in Leipzig, had become accentuated by chronic catarrh and bronchitis. The Westland climate, with its cold and fogs, was deadly to a man in his condition, as Grieg well knew; but he could not bring himself to abandon Troldhaugen and his beloved mountains. There was almost an understanding, he felt, between him and them. An entry in his diary, made on the 31st July 1906, explains his steadfastness in the face of reason: "The Westland is a love that costs me dear, for it robs me of my life. But it was the Westland that gave me life, the thrill of life, the desire to reproduce it in sound. The gift has really been a loan. I must pay it back when it falls due."

The few compositions belonging to these years help to discharge the obligation, for they all "reproduce in sound" the spirit of the mountains, both in its natural and its human aspects. The set of seven pieces called *Stemninger* ("Moods") (op. 73), which was published in 1905 and may be regarded as a supplement to the ten books of *Lyric Pieces*, contains a folk-tune from Valders

and a *Lualaat* ("Mountaineer's Song") of singu-
larly haunting character. But the most interesting
of all Grieg's piano works is unquestionably the
Slaatter or Peasant Dance Tunes (op. 72) which
appeared three years earlier.

As far back as 1889, and again in 1890, Grieg
received letters[1] from Knut Dale, who claimed to
be one of the last of the traditional players of
slaatter on the Hardanger fiddle, an instrument
equipped, like the old *viola d'amore*, with sym-
pathetic strings under the finger board, and tuned
in a variety of ways. In a series of quaint, rambling
letters Knut Dale addressed himself to Grieg as
"our land's greatest musician" to enquire if the
tunes he had learnt by rote from famous players
like Møllergutten and Gibøen could be noted
down and printed, and thus preserved for posterity. Grieg seems to have answered Dale's earlier
letter non-committally, but the old man was per-
sistent and wrote again in October, 1901 whereupon Grieg replied that while his own interest in
the tunes was genuine, he was too ill and too busy
to undertake to visit Dale in his home in remote
Telemarken; he felt, too, that only a skilled
violinist could make a satisfactory transcript of the
slaatter, played as they were with all the subtle
embellishments of the traditional style. He pro-
mised to enlist the help of a violinist in Christiania,
and to see if the money could be found to pay
Dale's expenses for a journey to the capital. On
the same day he wrote to Johan Halvorsen,
Director of Music at the National Theatre, pro-
posing that Halvorsen should transcribe the tunes

[1] For the whole correspondence, see Norsk Musikkgranskning Årbok
1943–6.

in the first place, that he himself should then make an arrangement for piano, and that both versions should be published by Peters. Halvorsen at once agreed to play his part, and Grieg arranged for the aged Dale to make his first journey from home for thirty years.

In the course of a lively correspondence Halvorsen kept Grieg posted with regard to the progress of the work. He said that he was having trouble over the notation of the trills and flourishes that resembled "a little trout in a rapid. As one tries to capture them they are gone." He is delighted with some of the rhythmic features of the tunes Dale plays him—"a mixture of 2/4 and 6/8 time that made me laugh aloud with glee". He also hints at the old man's propensity for demanding additional "expenses" and his reputation for indulging in the Norse equivalent of "one over the eight"—though, as Grieg remarks, "he wouldn't be a true fiddler if he were not fond of Bacchus". The dance-tunes Dale produced were mainly specimens of the *gangar* (walking dance) and *springdans* (leaping dance), with some bridal marches. After a fortnight's sessions Halvorsen had taken down seventeen tunes, tried to straighten out Knut Dale's involved finances, and sent him home. By the 6th of December the violin transcripts of the *slaatter* were in Grieg's hands, with a covering letter from Halvorsen commenting on points of technical interest in the tunes, such as the frequent occurrence of the sharpened fourth of the scale. Grieg replied from Troldhaugen in a typically warm and enthusiastic letter:

"I call this a real Saturday evening, dear Halvorsen. Outside rages a storm that shakes the house, while a regular deluge pours down from the heavens. But indoors it is cosy. I have just got your *slaatter* and read them through, fairly clucking with pleasure the while. All the same, I have been fuming at not being a fiddler. How I still hate that Conservatory at Leipzig!— But to the matter in hand. What you describe as "remarkable"—the use of a G sharp in the scale of D major—was the same thing that thrilled me in the year 1871. Of course I stole it in my *Pictures of Folk Life*. That note is a subject for research. The sharpened fourth can also be heard in folk-songs. It is a ghost from some old scale or other. But which? It is incomprehensible that we have no one turning his attention to research into national music, though we have in our folk-music these new sources for those who have ears to hear with, hearts to feel with, and the brains to write down.

"At present it seems to me a sin to arrange the *slaatter* for piano. But it's a sin I shall have to commit sooner or later. It's too tempting. I must thank you most heartily for your work; it has given me enormous pleasure and the future will show that it has done more than that. I can scarcely undertake this job before the summer. Would you like me, when the time comes, to try and get both your work and mine brought out by Peters?"

With his usual honesty Grieg insisted that this should be done. The publishers must show on the title page that Halvorsen's transcriptions were the original ones, and Grieg's piano arrangements based on those. Grieg was right when he said that only a violinist could have taken down the tunes in the first place from the Hardanger fiddle and adapt them for the ordinary violin. But if one compares the Halvorsen version with Grieg's piano version of the *Slaatter* (op. 72) one realises that in their pianistic form they are virtually new creations. Never before had Grieg's harmony been so bold, his rhythms so complex, his treatment of the piano so uncompromisingly percussive. In all these respects the *Slaatter* are prophetic of Bartók; and it is a measure of their audacity that they have remained almost unknown for nearly half a century while Grieg's piano pieces have been dismissed by facile critics as sugary drawing-room confections. Some of those to whom Grieg's name suggests nothing more than the earlier (and easier) *Lyric Pieces* are likely to be shocked and repelled by the *Slaatter*, which spare neither performer nor listener. But to those of a robust musical constitution these are among the most stimulating pieces in modern pianoforte literature.

The *Slaatter* appeared in print in the early months of 1903. This was a busy year. There were concerts in Prague (where the diminutive master was overwhelmed with "wreaths of silver, laurel, and palm, as big as mill-wheels"), in Warsaw, and in Paris, where, as we have seen, occurred the sequel to the "Dreyfus" letter.

In June there were celebrations of the composer's sixtieth birthday, with the Bjørnsons and Julius Röntgen as guests of honour. The more public part of the festivities included a reception on the 15th at Troldhaugen, a banquet on the 16th where Bjørnson made one of his most eloquent speeches, setting the whole of Grieg's life-work against a rugged background of nature and tradition in Norway, and on the 17th an excursion to the neighbouring mountains, in which the whole of the orchestra of the National Theatre, and many other artists, were regally entertained at the composer's expense. On each night also there were concerts—the first two in the National Theatre in Bergen and the last in the open air. On the 15th the programme included the "Homage March" from *Sigurd Jorsalfar*, the Piano Concerto, two transcriptions for strings—"The First Meeting" and "The Last Spring", the song "Henrik Wergeland" (op. 58, no. 3) with orchestra, "The Mountain Thrall", and the first *Peer Gynt* Suite ("the inevitable", as Grieg remarked). The composer conducted, the singer was Ingolf Schiøtt, and the pianist Elizabeth Hals-Anderssen. The concert was rounded off with a setting of Bjørnson's poem "To Bergen" by Halvorsen, and Grieg then made a speech from a balcony of the theatre. The first half of the second night's programme consisted of Norwegian works: Sinding's *Rondo infinito*, Grieg's *Bridal Procession* orchestrated by Halvorsen, two excerpts from Halvorsen's music to Bjørnson's *The King*, Svendsen's *Carnival in Paris*, and Grieg's Overture *In Autumn*. In the second half the orchestra played Beethoven's Overture *Leonore* No. 3, a Liszt Hungarian Rhapsody, and some Wagner excerpts.

Grieg entered whole-heartedly into the spirit of

all this; he was never happier than when he had
true friends and admirers about him, and he had
all the Scandinavian fondness for a festive occasion.
But reaction followed; for the rest of the summer
he was prostrated with nervous exhaustion and
with sleeplessness caused by bouts of asthma.
Some weeks in the Bergen hospital, and in health
resorts in the mountains helped to bring about a
partial recovery, but it seemed wiser to leave
Troldhaugen in September and pass the winter in
the drier climate of Christiania.

He returned to the Westland for the summer of
1904, in time for an experience that gave him a
good deal of pleasure although he was, as he told
his German publishers, little *hoffähig*. The Kaiser
Wilhelm II, who since 1889 had taken a fancy to
spending summer vacations in Norway, in this
year had his yacht moored in Bergen harbour,
complete with the imperial private orchestra—it
may be remembered that he was an amateur composer and conductor of some pretensions. He
expressed a wish to meet Grieg, and the composer
was summoned to a breakfast at the German consul's. Grieg was completely at his ease conversing
on "poetry, painting, religion, socialism and
goodness knows what else", and then the orchestra
of forty players was assembled to play the *Sigurd*
and *Peer Gynt* music and other examples of Grieg's
work. In one of his picturesque letters the composer describes how the Kaiser sat beside him "and
during the music constantly urged me to correct
the tempi and interpretation, although this naturally had not been my intention. He desired me
throughout, however, to make my wishes known.

He then illustrated the effect of the music by movements of the head and body. 'Anitra's Dance' quite electrified him, and it was marvellous to see his serpentine convolutions in the manner of an oriental maiden." After the orchestral items Grieg was made to sit down at the piano; he played the minuet from the Piano Sonata, which the Kaiser found "sehr germanisch und mächtig aufgebaut" and his "Wedding Day at Troldhaugen" (op. 65, no. 6). The following day Grieg was invited to dinner in the yacht *Hohenzollern* where the orchestra played on deck, while hundreds of people in rowing boats and small motor craft gathered round to listen. The Kaiser was solicitous for Grieg's health and wrapped him in his own cloak, waxing enthusiastic the while as Grieg told him the plot of *Sigurd Jorsalfar*, and declaring that it must be performed in Berlin. Altogether, Grieg was much impressed by the Kaiser's personality: "He liked children and animals and was fond of speaking of them, and that is an important sign." Whether the Kaiser was genuinely musical he prefers to leave as an open question.

In this, as in his other contacts with members of the then numerous royal houses of Europe, Grieg combined an engaging ease of manner with a certain reserve becoming in an artist. He tells us little of his command performance, with Nina, before Queen Victoria in 1898; but an amusing letter to Hinrichsen (29th June 1906) describes his reaction to the Court manners of King Edward VII: ". . . . While I was playing to him, as he had requested, he talked so loudly that twice I had to stop. But the best of the story is in the sequel.

The King and Queen had asked us to bear their greetings to the King and Queen of Norway, and we were therefore obliged to pay the latter a visit. As you know, our King is quite approachable and when we came to speak of the King of England I told him good-humouredly about his talkativeness. 'Yes,' said the King, who apparently wanted to defend his father-in-law, 'but I must tell you that the King of England can talk and listen to music at the same time! . . .' Rather good, wasn't it? All I said was: 'That may be so,' (though it isn't), 'but it is not allowed, even for the King of England, and for the sake of my art I cannot overlook it.' Whereupon the King shrugged his shoulders in a humorous way and gave a kindly smile. In short, he is a very kindly person, and it's all the more regrettable that he appears to have absolutely no understanding of music."

We have already seen how anxiously Grieg watched the political situation in 1905. His letters to Hinrichsen during the critical period are full of it: "In Sweden, as in Norway, it is hoped that everything will be solved without bloodshed. The contrary would be a crime unparalleled. We are, however, fortunately prepared and for this reason Sweden will probably take care not to attack us. It is a serious, weighty, and decisive time for Norway" (29th May) . . . "The nations are horrified at the idea of war. Only a small party in the Swedish Government is egging the King on and seems to be possessed with megalomania. Well, we hope for the best. Our Government is splendid and has the confidence of the

whole people." (14th June) . . . "Should the
Swedes commit the nameless crime of attacking us
there would come a dreadful time for Norway.
We should fight like the Japanese, just as fanatic-
ally to the last man. The worst and greatest mis-
fortune is that the Norwegian nation is a young
one, whereas the Swedish is a middle-aged one.
The conflict is thus unavoidable. With us it is the
nation itself that rules, in Sweden a few hidden
aristocrats with antediluvian opinions" (25th June).
. . . "I have had to give up the concerts in Fin-
land, to which I was invited, since I cannot travel
through Sweden. It sounds incredible, but chauvinism has gone so far in that country that they are
driving out Norwegians who have been staying
there, will not perform the works of Bjørnson, and
reject my compositions with hisses and other
demonstrations, while we treat those of Sweden
with the utmost politeness. You see which nation
represents the healthy attitude in this respect.
But more—you see in this an indication which is
right. People only behave as the Swedes are now
behaving if they are *wrong*. Well, it is the Press
that has ruined the nation and must bear the
blame." (28th August) . . . Even the Treaty of
Karlstad, signed on the 23rd of September, did not
altogether allay his anxiety; he considered that the
terms imposed on his country by Sweden were
harsh and vindictive. But gratitude gained the
upper hand; though a confirmed republican, he
welcomed the accession of Haakon VII, took part
in the national rejoicings on the 28th November
when *Sigurd Jorsalfar* was performed at the
National Theatre, and both Grieg and Bjørnson

were presented to the new King and Queen, and
on the 31st December wrote in his diary: "Now
passes the year 1905, the great year, to its rest, and
I part from it in deep thankfulness that I lived to
see it."[1] There is perhaps little wonder that this
year produced no original composition, except for
the album of *Moods* (op. 73) for piano. Apart
from Grieg's preoccupation with the political crisis
his considerable international reputation brought
with it many business cares. Publishers had to be
written to, earlier editions brought up to date,
concert engagements accepted or declined, legal
matters—like the revision of international copyright laws—dealt with. All this labour was dis-
charged, not merely with competence, but with
humour and humanity; those are the qualities
that inform every page of his vast correspondence.

The inner circle of his friends was enlarged in
1906 by the admission of Percy Grainger, to whom
we have already referred as a member of some
mountain expeditions. Grainger was then twenty-
four, and first attracted Grieg's attention in
London during May of that year by playing the
piano versions of the *Slaatter* with an insight that
delighted the composer beyond measure. Grainger seemed to have an innate sympathy for Norwegian culture; as early as 1907, when he appeared
in Norway and joined Grieg, Beyer, and Röntgen
in the mountains, he had learnt to speak Norse
(and also Icelandic and Faroesk) fluently. He had
also begun to make phonograph recordings of
English folk-tunes, specimens of which he brought
with him. Among these was doubtless the famous

[1] Johansen, *op. cit.* English translation, p. 358.

recording of Joseph Taylor singing "Brigg Fair",
the tune that inspired Delius—also a friend of
Grieg's—to write his well-known Rhapsody. It is
interesting to recall that in 1899 both Edvard and
Nina Grieg had been invited to become honorary
members of the newly formed Folk-Song Society,
and that some six years later Grieg wrote to Percy
Grainger: "I admire the way in which the Society
is organised and grieve that my Fatherland so rich
in folk material cannot boast such an organisation.
. . . I am impressed by the earnestness and energy
with which the English (*sic*) Folk-Song Society
carries out its object. May it ever enjoy fresh
increase of strength and enthusiasm to pursue its
goal!"[1]

Grainger was to be closely connected with the
last stages of Grieg's life as man and artist. Not
only did he give the *Slaatter* a better reading, as
Grieg admitted, than any Norwegian pianist had
succeeded in doing, and had been chosen to play
the solo part in the Piano Concerto at the ill-fated
Leeds concert in September 1907, but he stood
sponsor to Grieg's last groups of compositions—the
Four Psalms for mixed voices (op. 74).

In Grieg's diary occurs the following entry for the
15th September: "Completed 3 Psalms for mixed
choir and soli, free arrangements from Lindeman's Norwegian Folk-tunes. They are so
beautiful, these melodies, that they deserve to be
cherished in an artistic setting. These small works
are the only ones my wretched health has allowed
me to carry out in the course of the summer
months. The feeling that 'I would, if only I

[1] Journal of the English Folk Dance and Song Society, vol. v, no. 3, December
1948; Article, *The Folk-Song Society*, 1898–1948, by Frederick Keel.

could' is enough to drive one to despair. I fight in vain against odds and must soon give up altogether." . . . Early in December he wrote to Beyer, telling him that the fourth Psalm was finished, and a week or so later he offered them to Peters for publication, suggesting that he might have them translated into German by Cläre Mjoen, the translator of Bjørnson's works. The English translation was made by Percy Grainger, who also contributed a Foreword describing the *Psalms* as "outpourings of that rare devotional mood previously manifested in (Grieg's) 'I walk with a thousand thoughts' (Adagio religioso, op. 66, no. 18) and 'The Great White Host' ('Den store hvide Flok') op. 30, no. 15. On the technical side this last opus carries on the iconoclastic achievements of his *Album for Male Voices* (op. 30). Both volumes are remarkable for the masterly manner in which highly original and daring complexities of chromatic and enharmonic polyphonic harmony are couched in a perfectly vocal and naturally singable style . . . thereby, for the first time, making the harmonic innovations of the latter 19th century available for choral use. It is this side of Grieg's compositional technique . . . that has so profoundly influenced modern Anglo-Saxon choral writing. In proving the applicability and effectiveness of post-Wagnerian polyphonic harmonies to, and in vocal composition, Grieg has given an impetus to choral music that was lacking throughout the major part of the 19th century . . ." These claims may seem a little overstated; but in relation to modern English choral music at least there is a good deal of truth in them. Grainger is obviously thinking chiefly of the works of Delius, and of his own choral settings. Delius was profoundly, and consciously, influenced by Grieg, and in his turn set a fashion for smooth but highly chromatic choral polyphony that many younger writers in England were glad to follow. Even at the present time it cannot be said to have lost all its potency.

Of the chorales chosen by Grieg for these settings, the first two—"Hvad est du dog skjön" ("How fair is Thy face") and "Guds Sön har gjort mig fri" ("God's Son hath set me free") have words by the eighteenth-century Danish bishop and religious poet, H. A. Brorson. The other two— "Jesus Kristus er opfaren" ("Jesus Christ is risen") and "I Himmelen" ("In Heaven") go back to the sixteenth century. The melodies of all four are traditional and probably of folk origin; for the Norwegian Reformed Church, while drawing for its hymnology partly upon the common Lutheran stock, has adapted to religious use a number of native tunes of distinctive beauty. In the first Psalm we see how Grieg applies his techniques of folk-song arrangement to the chorale, giving it first to a bass soloist with an accompaniment of reiterated chords, and later developing it in free, flowing counterpoint that keeps closely to the modal lines of the tune. Diatonic progressions, bold and often dissonant, predominate. The climax (at the words "All that I have is Thine!") is particularly strong and satisfying. In the second Psalm there are even more exhilarating harmonic experiments; the confident major tonality of the chorale is combined with accompanying progressions in the minor mode, so that a strange and arresting kind of symbolism is produced by purely musical means. In the third Psalm solo and response are used in the manner of a liturgical setting, and there is a rhythmic freedom that comes, with the chorale itself, from the sixteenth century. "In Heaven" is another sturdy, uncomplicated expression of Protestant faith, and Grieg's treatment of it has a freshness whose childlike quality one can best realise by trying to imagine what Brahms or Mahler, each in his own way, would have done with such material. In one of his last letters Grieg told his friend, the Swiss Pastor L. Monastier-Schroeder, how he had been attracted by the teachings of the Unitarians during his first visit to England in 1888, and had found all religious problems resolved by them once and for all. "Nothing that has since been urged upon me has made any impression." An unaffected and steadfast piety is revealed constantly in his letters, but reaches its finest and fullest expression in the *Four Psalms*. From the spiritual standpoint, these works are a remarkable testament of faith and devotion. From the artistic standpoint, they show the composer, at the very end of his career, applying to new purposes a technique and style that have been refined and controlled by a lifetime of experiment and self-criticism.

The *Psalms* appeared in print but a few days after Grieg's death. They reflect faithfully and touchingly one side of his nature; but they do not give us the whole picture of Grieg as a human being, even during these final months. Ill though he was, he was wonderfully active throughout his last year. His letters are full of varied and interesting happenings: there is Amundsen's return in November 1906 from his victory over the North-West Passage, th ere are Brahms's letters to the Herzogenbergs to be read as a bed-book, there is a matinee concert in Copenhagen to be conducted at the request of his friend and fellow-townsman, Dr. Armauer-Hansen, discoverer of the leprosy bacillus; the proceeds of the concert are to be devoted to a hospital for the disease in the West Indies. Röntgen came over in February 1907, and gave in Christiania a number of concerts, one of which was attended by the King and Queen of Norway. On this occasion Grieg played with Röntgen his *Norwegian Dances* for piano duet, and accompanied Nina, who now rarely sang in public; it was to be their last appearance together on a concert platform. Röntgen's visit ended with a banquet which Grieg arranged in his honour. "What a host he was", Röntgen wrote in his memoirs. "How well he understood how to cheer a guest and put him in a good humour! He began with a long speech about me, and ended with a Norwegian 'hurrah' which he 'conducted'." Later in the spring, there were concerts in Copenhagen, Munich, Berlin and Kiel. "It was very sad for me to think that I had conducted in Germany for the last time", Grieg wrote at the beginning of May. "In Berlin I was invited to lunch with the Kaiser and there I met Massenet and Saint-Saëns. But as I couldn't speak French the situation was a little difficult. I also met Richard Strauss."

On his way back from Kiel Grieg stayed in Copenhagen for light-baths and other treatment.

He felt weak and depressed and could do no work. Offers of spectacular contracts from America touch his old vein of whimsicality: "The irony of fate!" he writes to Hinrichsen, "America wants to make a rich man of me. No thank you. Thanks of quite another kind I owe to you and Dr. Abraham for making it possible for me to enjoy an old age free from material cares. My gratitude will never end as long as I can breathe."

In the summer Grainger and Röntgen were, as we have seen, visitors to Troldhaugen. Grieg seemed to have rallied, and enjoyed the days of walking and music-making with his friends; but in seeing Röntgen off by boat from Bergen Grieg spoke a last farewell: "I feel and know that we shall not see each other again. My strength is at an end and it cannot last longer. We must say good-bye for ever." Then, says Röntgen, "I saw Grieg step into his carriage and I went, deeply moved, towards my cabin. I was startled out of my sad thoughts by the thunder of cannon from the neighbouring fort—the salute of the German Kaiser, who was in the *Hohenzollern* in Bergen Harbour."

Yet Grieg continued to make his plans for a journey to England, where at the Leeds Festival in October he was to conduct *Scenes from Olav Trygvason* and the Piano Concerto with Grainger as soloist. It had been arranged that the first stage of the journey should be from Troldhaugen to Christiania, by way of Bergen and Laerdal. On Monday, 2nd September, the Griegs drove to the Hotel Norge, in Bergen, where they were to spend the night before taking the steamer for Laerdal.

Everyone noticed how ill Grieg was looking; he could scarcely stand or speak, and on the following day his doctor declared that he must be taken to the Bergen Hospital. The end came in the early hours of the 4th September, and its manner can best be told in the grief-stricken words of Nina: "He suffered terribly from breathlessness but in the end, thank God, fell asleep as calmly as a child. In my unspeakable anxiety the doctor had sent me away on the last night, and when I had been fetched I found him lifeless. I was with him in the sickroom until half past eleven. . . . Forgive me, Herr Hinrichsen, but I can no longer think in a foreign tongue. . . ." Death was due to heart failure, caused by exhaustion from the excessive strain imposed by a collapsed lung.

The funeral ceremonies held publicly in Bergen on the 9th September must have recalled to many onlookers those that had attended the passing of Ole Bull twenty-seven years earlier. In the hall of the Westland Museum of Industrial Art a large orchestra, led by the Russian violinist Brodsky and conducted by Halvorsen, played *The Last Spring* and the Nordraak Funeral March, and a male-voice choir, with Ingolf Schiøtt as soloist, sang "The Great White Host" from the *Album for Male Voices*. It was in keeping with the character of the man they mourned for, and of the democratic nation to which he belonged, that in a great concourse of distinguished people from all over Europe the funeral oration should have been pronounced by Grieg's doctor and personal friend, Dr. Klaus Hanssen.

The body was cremated, and the following

spring, on the 4th April 1908, the ashes were deposited by Frants Beyer in a grotto cut in the rock face overlooking the fjord near Troldhaugen. The place is marked by the composer's name carved in letters of runic pattern.

Nina lived on through a vigorous old age, secure in the memory of a happy partnership. For another quarter of a century she kept up old friendships, played and sang her old songs—Schubert, Schumann, and Grieg—and answered enquiries about her husband's life and works. In a note written in 1931, she complains of failing eyesight and weariness: "I am so old—85! I have to do more than I really can manage. There are so many of Grieg's admirers in the world. They all want autographs. Soon I shall have no more." She died in Copenhagen towards the end of 1935, a few days after her ninetieth birthday.

POSTSCRIPT

APART from the handicap of chronic ill health there was no great disharmony between Grieg's life as a man and as an artist. His was an attractive, well-balanced personality, with a natural capacity for making and keeping friends, to whom he liked to express himself in his letters in a way that was frank and intimate without being in the least degree morbidly self-analytical. Ready sympathy, quick intelligence, vivid imagination, and a keen wit, rather than intellectual brilliance and grasp, are the distinguishing qualities of his mind, and similar qualities are to be found in his music.

Looking at the music as a whole, one is struck by the high proportion that belongs to the best of its kind. Popularity is here not altogether the surest guide. The honest admirer of the composer will be ready to admit that better theatre music has been written than the *Sigurd Jorsalfar* entractes, better perhaps than is to be found in the *Peer Gynt* Suites; that the violin and cello sonatas are not to be compared with those of Brahms or Fauré; that the choral works are undistinguished except for the *Album for Male Voices* and the *Four Psalms*—though these are notable exceptions. He will be less willing to yield the claims of the Piano Concerto to be one of the most satisfying works of its class written during the nineteenth century or those of the *Elegiac Melodies* and the *Holberg* Suite to be indispensable contributions to the repertory of the string orchestra. But about the two largest sections of Grieg's output there can hardly be any dispute; his short pieces for piano are as much a part of the minor literature of the instrument as the mazurkas of Chopin, the *Songs without Words* of Mendelssohn, the *Scenes of Childhood* and *Papillons* of Schumann, and the *Intermezzi* of Brahms. It is true that many of them are slight in content and obvious in construction—the latter at least a criticism that can be made of some of the other works just mentioned. But there is scarcely one that does not manage to say something fresh, and to say it in an idiom that is thoroughly pianistic. As for the songs, of which Grieg published about a hundred and forty, they are *sui generis*. It is both unjust and unprofitable to attempt to compare them with the great German *lieder*. They are mainly in strophic form and seldom range over the gamut of the emotions in a way that is the essence of the true *lied*; like the songs of Fauré, with which they have much more in common than they have with the songs of Schubert, Schumann, and Wolf, they are essentially lyrical, reflecting a picture or mood in carefully wrought vocal phrases and exquisite pianoforte accompaniments. One is reminded again and again of the composer's remarks (already quoted) on the nature of poetic expression in Norwegian literature: "The stormy ocean of the passions is felt rather than glimpsed." His success in song-writing was, of course, bound up with his good fortune in having Nina as his interpreter; their partnership began with the Andersen songs of op. 5, and when Nina ceased to sing in public—about 1900—the fountain of song also disappears.

Although—or perhaps because—his style was strongly individual Grieg exerted considerable influence on other composers. Many of these were minor figures of the calibre of Edward Mac-Dowell; but more important men—Debussy, Ravel, Delius, Sibelius—each in his own way owes something to Grieg. Through Debussy and Ravel the impressionism of Grieg's later piano works, and his harmonic idiom in general flowed into the stream of French impressionism. Ravel once asserted that all his works had been influenced by the Norwegian composer. The chromatic harmony that is so marked a feature of the style of Delius is far closer to the chromaticism of Grieg than to that of Wagner; and the English composer's affection for progressions of secondary sevenths and ninths and other diatonic discords also reflects his admiration of the harmonic mannerisms of Grieg. In several cases—*Eventyr*, for example, *Paa Vidderne*, the two sets of *Songs from the Norwegian*, and *On hearing the first cuckoo*, Delius took a programme, verses, or even a folk-tune quotation from Norwegian sources. Through Delius, Grainger, and Peter Warlock, the Griegian influence was transmitted to a number of composers of the Georgian period. Bax's *Hardanger*, and several of his smaller pieces for piano solo, bear marks of this influence.

Sibelius is a less obvious case than any of those so far mentioned. It might seem that nothing could be more remote from Grieg's exquisitely worked miniatures than the vast monumental structures of Sibelius. But there is a lesser Sibelius, to be found in some of his entractes for the theatre and in the little piano pieces, that seems to belong to the Scandinavian side of his ancestry rather than to the Finnish, and comes very close in character to the *Holberg* Suite, "Anitra's Dance", and certain of the *Lyric Pieces*. Conversely, as the strange little movement for strings and horns that precedes Act IV of *Peer Gynt* and is not included in either of the orchestral suites might almost be taken for a page of Sibelius. Even in Sibelius's larger works—*The Swan of Tuonela, Tapiola*, parts of the symphonies—there are echoes of Grieg in tonality, harmony, and instrumental treatment—particularly, under the last heading, in the laying-out of passages for strings.

Over later Norwegian composers Grieg's influence was, as might be expected so strong as to produce eventually a reaction against the romanticism of his earlier works and against his consistent use of folk-tune; but even a contemporary writer like Harald Saeverud has not escaped—assuming perhaps impertinently that he would have wished to escape—the influence of last period Grieg. Whether as original a composer as Fartein Valen acknowledges any debt to Grieg is more doubtful, but it is interesting to remember that Valen's atonalism is fundamentally distinct from Schönberg's, and originated at an earlier date. We may have here a development of Grieg's exploitation of various diatonic and chromatic tonalities.

Grieg's discovery, through Ole Bull, Kjerulf, Nordraak, and finally Lindeman, of the rich treasury of Norwegian folk-song was opportune for the flowering of his musical personality. It is not always realised, however, how far he was already predisposed towards the idioms of folk-music. His interest in scales other than the classical major and minor, in traits like the sharpened fourth and flattened seventh of the scale, in ornamentation of a particularly elusive kind that produces piquant but transitory discords, in the liberal use of pedal-notes, in chords built up by fourths as well as thirds, in brief, reiterated melodic motives—all this was undoubtedly strengthened by contact with Norwegian folk-music, which is full of such implications. But the same characteristics are found in the folk-music of other peoples, and in particular of a people that had already produced a composer of international reputation, with a strong racial idiom forming not an excrescence on his style but an integral element of it. Grieg's admiration for the music of Chopin began in his childhood, survived the disparaging attitude of his Leipzig professors, and coloured his earliest piano compositions. Taking a broad view of European music in the first half of the nineteenth century, we can see the racial characteristics of Chopin's music as well as Grieg's as symptomatic of a tendency— arising probably from complex political, social and artistic causes—to draw fresh energy from the primitive but richly varied song and dance of peasant communities. The tendency is strongest with musicians of Slavonic origin: Chopin, the Pole, Smetana, the Czech, and the Russian school that followed Glinka. Now Grieg was cut off by circumstances from some of its most vital manifestations, he seems to have known little of what the Russian nationalists (with the exception of Tchaikovsky, the least national of them all) were trying to do, and the fact that *Olav Trygvason* and *Boris Godounov* were contemporary is one of the intriguing coincidences of history. But he was peculiarly sensitive to the artistic climate of his time. It will be recalled that Liszt, at a comparatively early stage in Grieg's career, recognised in him an exponent of the nationalist tendencies that he saw developing all over Europe, and in which he himself did not disdain to share.

Grieg's treatment of folk-tune illustrates the integrity that is one of the leading traits of his artistic personality. It is never self-conscious, as with Liszt, or banal, as with Tchaikovsky, or condescending, as with some English composers who followed the folk-song fashion. Grieg always believes with all his heart in the worth of the melodies he borrows or arranges. He brings out their most characteristic beauties and then leaves them alone.

When, in 1869, Grieg first became acquainted with Lindeman's collection he had already composed a series of instrumental works including the Piano Sonata, the first two Violin Sonatas, and the Piano Concerto that follow dutifully, as far as their main plan of construction is concerned, the practice of the Leipzig school. That is to say, in the number, types, and order of their movements, in their fulfilment of the traditional routine of exposition, development, and recapitulation they

conform to a pattern, which is nothing more than
the husk of what was once the living organism of
classical sonata form. We know that Grieg was
not happy with this convention, but tried to adopt
it in deference to his teachers at Leipzig and to
Gade. His thematic material in these works is
generally picturesque and though never consisting
in quotation or adaptation of folk-tune is generally
tinged with its qualities. The organisation of the
movement as a whole, the ordering of its key-
system, the construction of passages and episodes,
the organic development of material, is clearly of
secondary interest to him. One is continually
being reminded of the old gibe against the use of
folk-tune in composition; that having stated a
melody, all the composer can do with it is to say it
over again louder. When the revelation of the full
range and diversity of folk-tune came to Grieg as
he pored over Lindeman's pages he seems to have
realised the futility of fighting against his own
inclinations. And so he came, reluctantly and
with a heavy heart, to the point of abandoning the
attempt to cast his thought in classical moulds. In
nothing is his artistic integrity more evident than
in taking this decision. As he matured he became
less capable of hack-work and note-spinning,
however respectable it might be in outward appearance and antecedents. When he could not bring
an idea to life he discarded it, as he did with the
second Piano Concerto and the Quintet and the
Peace Oratorio, or suppressed it, as he did with the
early Symphony. When a work that had been
published and popularised haunted him with a
sense of imperfection his fastidiousness made him

constantly revise and refashion; this, as we have
noted, happened with the *Peer Gynt* music, the
Autumn Overture, and the Piano Concerto.

Grieg liked to draw attention to his affinity with
the French spirit in music, as opposed to the
tendencies he found in some of his German contemporaries. Where a great part of Europe was
swept by enthusiasm for Wagnerism he stood fast
in his independent point of view and, while recog-
nising the stature of Wagner's genius, refused to
swallow whole all Wagner's theories or to be
carried away on the powerful tide of his sonority.
Grieg has a good title to be counted among the
leaders of the resistance movement against Wag-
nerian domination in the last quarter of the
nineteenth century—a leader who exercised his
influence rather by strength of conviction and
quiet example than by any violent programme of
opposition.

Although a minor figure in the story of modern
European music Grieg occupies a definite and
unassailable position. Belonging to a small country without artistic institutions such as the other
Scandinavian countries have long possessed, he
helped to release the powers of musical expression
latent in his countrymen. He brought Norway
into the stream of European music while enhancing
her individuality and his own. He bequeathed to
posterity not only a collection of musical works,
miniatures for the most part but of fine workman-
ship and original design, but also the memory of a
rich and lovable character.

BIBLIOGRAPHY (Selected)

In English:
Monrad-Johansen, D.: *Edvard Grieg* (Oslo, 1934; English trans. Madge Robertson, Princeton University Press, 1938).
Finck, H. T.: *Edvard Grieg* (London, 1906; second edn., with additions, 1929).
Abraham, G. (ed.): *Grieg: a Symposium* (*Music of the Masters*, London, 1948).
Mason, D. G.: *From Grieg to Brahms* (New York, 1902).
The Musical Times, October 1907 (Obituary article).
In Norwegian:
Breve fra Grieg (Copenhagen, 1922).
Breve fra Edvard Grieg til Frants Beyer (Christiania, 1923).
Schjelderup and Sandvik: *Norges Musikhistorie* (Christiania, 1921).
Norsk Musikkgranskning Årbok 1943–1946 (Oslo, 1947).
Greni, L.: *Rikard Nordraak* (Oslo, 1942).
Elling, C.: *Norsk Folkemusik* (Christiania, 1922).
In German:
Fischer, K. von: *Griegs Harmonik und die nordländische Folklore* (Berne and Leipzig, 1938).
Schjelderup and Niemann: *Edvard Grieg: Biographie und Würdigung seiner Werke* (Leipzig, 1908).
Stein, R.: *Grieg* (Berlin, 1921).
Briefe an die Verleger der Edition Peters, 1866–1907 (Leipzig, 1932).
In French:
Rokseth, Y.: *Grieg* (Paris, 1933).
de Stoecklin, P.: *Grieg* (Paris, 1926).
In Dutch and German:
Röntgen, J.: *Grieg* (The Hague, 1925).

LIST OF COMPOSITIONS

I. ORCHESTRAL WORKS

(a) FULL ORCHESTRA

Date of composition	Opus No.	Work
1864 (None: but see op. 14)		Symphony in C minor
1866, reorch. 1887	11	Concert Overture, *I Høst* (*In Autumn*)
1868, rev. 1906-7	16	Concerto in A minor for piano and orchestra
1874-5, rev. 1888	46	First *Peer Gynt* Suite
1891, orch. 1900	51	Old Norwegian Melody with Variations
1874-5, rev. 1891	55	Second *Peer Gynt* Suite
1872, rev. 1892	56	Three Pieces from *Sigurd Jorsalfar*
1898	64	Symphonic Dances

(b) STRING ORCHESTRA

1880, orch. 1881	34	Two Elegiac Melodies
1884, orch. 1885	40	Suite, *From Holberg's Time*
1880 and 1870, orch. 1891	53	Two Melodies: *Norsk* (Norwegian) and *Det Förste Möde* (The First Meeting)
1870, orch. 1895	63	Two Norwegian Melodies (*In Folk Style* and *Cow-call and Peasant Dance*)
1898	68 (no. 5)	*At the Cradle*
	68 (no. 4)	*Evening in the Mountains* (Strings, oboe, and horn)

(The last three items are Grieg's own arrangements of piano pieces; op. 34 and op. 53 are arrangements of songs.)

II. WORKS FOR THE STAGE

1872	22	Incidental Music to Bjørnson's *Sigurd Jorsalfar*
1874-5, reorch. 1886	23	Incidental Music to Ibsen's *Peer Gynt*

Date of composition	Opus No.	Work
1873, orch. 1889	50	Opera, *Olav Trygvason* (text by Bjørnson). (Unfinished)

III. WORKS FOR CHORUS AND ORCHESTRA

1871	20	*Foran Sydens Kloster* (At a Southern Convent's Gate), Female voices and orchestra.
1872	22	Two Songs from *Sigurd Jorsalfar*, Male voices and orchestra
1872, rev. 1881	31	*Landkjaending* (Recognition of Land), Male voices and orch., with organ ad lib.

IV. MELODRAMA

1871, orch. 1885	42	*Bergliot* (text by Bjørnson)

V. CHAMBER MUSIC

1865	8	Sonata No. 1 in F, violin and piano
1867	13	Sonata No. 2 in G, violin and piano
1877-8	27	String Quartet in G Minor
1883	36	Sonata in A minor, cello and piano
1887	45	Sonata No. 3 in C minor, violin and piano
1891	(None)	String Quartet in F (unfinished)

VI. SOLO SONGS

Before 1862	10	*Four Romances* (Christian Winther)
1862	2	*Four Songs for Alto* (Chamisso and Heine)
1863-4	4	*Six Songs* (Chamisso, Heine, Uhland)
1864	5	*Melodies of the Heart* (Andersen)
1864-5	9	*Romances and Ballads* (Andreas Munch)
1868, 1864, 1870	15	*Four Songs* (Ibsen, Andersen, Richardt)
1865-9	18	*Romances* (Andersen)
1870-2	21	*Four Songs* from *The Fishermaiden* (Bjørnson)
1876	25	*Six Songs* (Ibsen)
1876	26	*Five Songs* (J. Paulsen)
1878	32	*Den Bergtekne* (The Mountain Thrall) (Old Norse Ballad, for solo baritone string and horns)
1873-80	33	*Melodies* (A. O. Vinje)

Date of composition	Opus No.	Work
1870–85	39	Six Songs (Bjørnson, J. Lie, Richardt, Janson, O. P. Monrad, N. Rolfsen, after Heine)
1886	44	From Mountain and Fjord (H. Drachmann)
1889	48	Six Songs (Heine, Geibel, Uhland, W. von der Vogelweide, Goethe, Bodenstedt)
1889	49	Six Songs (Drachmann)
1894	58	Norge (Norway) (J. Paulsen)
1894	59	Elegiac Poems (J. Paulsen)
1894	60	Five Songs (V. Krag)
1894–5	61	Children's Songs (Rolfsen and others)
1896–8	67	Haugtussa Song-Cycle (A. Garborg)
1900	69	Five Songs (O. Benzon)
1900	70	Five Songs (O. Benzon)
1865	(None)	Dig elsker jeg (Thee I love) (Casalis)
1865	,,	Taaren (The Tear) and Soldaten (The Soldier) (Andersen)
1867	,,	Den Blonde pige (The fair maiden) (Bjørnson)
1870	,,	Odalisken synger (The odalisque sings) (C. Bruun)
1871	,,	Prinsessen (The Princess) (Bjørnson)
1873	,,	Suk (Sigh) (Bjørnson)
1880	,,	Paa Hamars Ruiner (Over Hamar's Ruins) (Vinje)
1889?	,,	Der Jäger (The Hunter) (Schultz) and Osterlied (Easter Song) (Böttger)
1889	,,	Simpel Sang (Simple Song) (Drachmann)
1891?	,,	Jeg elsket (I loved) (Bjørnson, from the oratorio Peace)
1899	,,	Ave Maris Stella
1900	,,	Julens Vuggesang (Christmas Lullaby) (Langsted)

VII. SHORTER CHORAL WORKS

1877–8	30	Album for Male Voices, freely arranged from Norwegian Folksongs
1906	74	Four Psalms

(Also a number of unpublished part-songs, choruses and cantatas for special occasions.)

VIII. PIANO WORKS (Two hands)

Date of composition	Opus No.	Work
1862	1	Four Piano Pieces
1863	3	Poetic Tone-Pictures
1866	(None)	Funeral March for Rikard Nordraak
1865	6	Humoresques
1865	7	Sonata in E minor
1867	12	Lyric Pieces, Book I
1870	17	Norwegian Songs and Dances
1872	19	Pictures of Folk-Life
1875	24	Ballad in the form of Variations on a Norwegian Folk-Tune
1875?	(None)	Six Norwegian Mountain Melodies
1864-8	28	Album Leaves
1878	29	Improvisations on Norwegian Folk-Tunes
1883	38	Lyric Pieces, Book II
1885	40	Suite, From Holberg's Time
1885	41	Song Transcriptions
1886	43	Lyric Pieces, Book III
1888	47	Lyric Pieces, Book IV
1891	52	Song Transcriptions
1891	54	Lyric Pieces, Book V
1893	57	Lyric Pieces, Book VI
1895	62	Lyric Pieces, Book VII
1896	65	Lyric Pieces, Book VIII
1896	66	Norwegian Folk-Tunes
1898	68	Lyric Pieces, Book IX
1901	71	Lyric Pieces, Book X
1902	72	Slaatter
1905	73	Stemninger (Moods)

Published posthumously, without opus no. *Three Piano Pieces* (White Clouds, Gnomes' Dance, The Dance Goes On—the first of these completed by Röntgen.)

(Piano Duet)		
1864	14	Two Symphonic Pieces (arrangement of movement from unpublished Symphony)
1881	35	Norwegian Dances
1883	37	Valses-caprices
1898	64	Symphonic Dances

(Two Pianos)		
1877	(None)	Additional parts for second piano to Mozart Piano Sonatas K533, K457, K475 (Fantasia), K545, K283
1891	51	Old Norwegian Melody with Variations

DATE DUE

GAYLORD | | | PRINTED IN U.S.A